MW00803134

N SCALE RAILROADING
Getting started in the hobby
— SECOND EDITION —

Marty McGuirk

KB
KALMBACH BOOKS

Kalmbach Books

21027 Crossroads Circle
Waukesha, WI 53186
www.kalmbach.com/books

© 2000, 2009 by Marty McGuirk
First edition published in 2000, Second edition in 2009

All rights reserved. Except for brief excerpts for review, this book may not be reproduced in part or in whole by electronic means or otherwise without written permission of the publisher.

Published in 2009
17 16 15 14 13   2 3 4 5 6

Manufactured in the United States of America

ISBN: 978-0-89024-773-0

Publisher's Cataloging-In-Publication Data

McGuirk, Martin J.
   N scale railroading : getting started in the hobby / Martin McGuirk. -- 2nd ed.

   p. : ill. (chiefly col.) ; cm. -- (Model railroader books)

   At head of title on cover: Model railroader's how-to guide
   ISBN: 978-0-89024-773-0

1. Railroads--Models--Handbooks, manuals, etc. 2. Railroads--Models--Design and construction. 3. Models and modelmaking. I. Title. II. Title: Model railroader's how-to guide III. Series: Model railroader books.

TF197 .M216 2009
625.1/9

Contents

1-1

CHAPTER ONE

N scale basics

The Maine Central in the 1970s and '80s was the prototype inspiration for the author's small N scale railroad. The author captured the railroad's colorful locomotives and the the spectacular colors of a New England autumn in creating a realistic layout.

Since it first appeared in 2000, *N Scale Model Railroading: Getting Started in the Hobby* has introduced thousands of model railroaders to the challenge and fun of model railroading in N scale. In the years since that book was written, the hobby has evolved and technology and products have improved dramatically. Some of the basic information in this volume is similar to that found in the earlier book (updated as necessary, of course), but there's a lot of new information between these covers. Perhaps the most obvious changes are the step-by-step chapters that walk you through building and operating a complete 4 x 8-foot N scale railroad.

1-2

N scale trains are accurately scaled to duplicate the dimensions and details of real full-size ("prototype") trains. Compare the prototype Maine Central GP38 in this photo to the Atlas N scale model shown in 1-1. *G.A. Pedick*

We felt it was time to show what an N scale modeler could do after successfully building a project like the Carolina Central, the door-sized layout featured in the first edition of the book. I'm continually pleased, and frankly amazed, by the number of model railroaders who send me e-mails and letters telling me the Carolina Central layout inspired them and provided the impetus to get them active in model railroad building.

In this book I've taken some of the tried-and-true methods that were so successful with the Carolina Central layout and combined them with some new and updated products and techniques. The result is the slightly more complex (but far more interesting to build and operate!) Androscoggin Central (**1-1**).

Although you could follow the steps in chapters 9, 10, and 11 and simply duplicate what I've done to build that layout, I'd be just as pleased to hear that the Androscoggin Central provided you with the inspiration to design and build your own layout based on your favorite railroad or location.

The purpose of that layout, and this book, is to help you get started by showing you all you need to know to build and operate your very own N scale empire. I've tried to answer the questions that I had when I got started in the hobby. I also asked several of my model railroading friends what questions they had. The results of this knowledge (some of it hard-earned!) is presented with the intent of helping you build a model railroad you can be proud of!

What is N scale?

N scale is one of the most popular indoor model railroad scales, second only to HO. And it's correctly referred to as "N scale," not "N gauge." There is a difference: Scale is the proportion of a model in relationship to the real thing. N scale has a ratio of 1:160; that is, each dimension of an N scale model is 1/160 of the real thing (**1-2**). "Gauge" refers to the distance between the rails. In the United States, Canada, and most of Europe, real trains run on tracks with the rails spaced 4' 8½" apart. This is referred to as "standard gauge."

The proportions in any given scale apply to buildings, automobiles, figures, trees, roads—everything on the layout. The chart in **1-3** shows some significant N scale dimensions.

Years ago many prototype railroads ("prototype" is what model railroaders call the real thing) were built with narrower track gauges. Three-foot gauge was the most common in the U.S., although a few railroads in Maine had a gauge of two feet. Model railroaders refer to these narrow gauge railroads using the scale followed by the small letter "n" (for narrow) and the track gauge in feet. So HOn3 means HO scale (1:87 proportion), 3-foot gauge. Narrow gauge modeling is not as common in N scale, although a few N scalers have built Nn3 layouts, using Z scale mechanisms and track, and Micro-Trains offers some rolling stock.

N scale is roughly half the size of the most popular scale, HO (1:87 proportion). The largest of the common indoor scales is O, which is 1:48 proportion, and large scale trains (from 1:20 to 1:32) are common in gardens and are sometimes used for indoor

Conversion chart

Prototype dimension in inches	N scale equivalent dimension in inches	Prototype dimension in inches/feet	N scale equivalent dimension in inches
¹⁄₆₄	.0001	4¼	.02656
¹⁄₃₂	.00019	4½	.02812
¹⁄₁₆	.00039	5	.03125
⅛	.00078	5¼	.03281
¼	.00156	5½	.03437
⅜	.00234	6	.0375
½	.00312	6¼	.03906
⅝	.0039	6½	.04062
¾	.00468	7	.04375
⅞	.00546	8	.05
1	.00625	9	.05625
1⅛	.00703	10	.0625
1¼	.00781	11	.06875
1⅜	.00859		
1½	.00937		
1⅝	.01015	1'	.075
1¾	.01093	2'	.15
1⅞	.01171	3'	.225
2	.0125	4'	.30
2¼	.01406	5'	.375
2½	.01562	6'	.45
3	.01875	7'	.525
3¼	.02031	8'	.60
3½	.02187	9'	.675
4	.025	10'	.75

Here's an example of how to use this table. Find the N scale equivalent of 5' 6¹⁵⁄₁₆".

Prototype	5' 0"	=	.375" in N scale
	6"	=	.0375"
	⅞"	=	.00546"
	¹⁄₁₆"	=	.00039"
	5' 6¹⁵⁄₁₆"	=	.41835"

1-3

model railroads. You can see a comparison of models in the various scales in **1-4**.

I've enjoyed building models and layouts in several scales, so I'm not a scale zealot who will try to convince you N scale is "best." I don't think there is one "best" scale, although each scale offers its advantages. If you want to build highly detailed models, you'll have an easier time of it in HO or O than N. However, if your goal is to create the appearance of a long train snaking its way through the countryside, it's hard to top N scale (**1-5**).

The key is to work within the opportunities and limitations of the scale. Don't let anyone tell you it's impossible to build realistic models in N scale. It may require different techniques and materials, but it's no more difficult to build a realistic model in N than any other scale. In fact, since we don't have to include every individual rivet, grab iron, and piece of underbody piping on our cars to create a realistic scene, it may actually be a little easier.

There has been an explosion in both the quality and quantity of N scale products in the past decade. Years ago

we were thrilled simply to have passenger cars—now we have specific models of cars that ran in several big-name trains.

If HO leads in both popularity and equipment availability, why bother with N scale? The primary and most obvious reason is that N scale takes up so much less space than HO. This means you can build an N scale layout in an area about 30 percent the size of a comparable HO layout. Many starter HO layouts are built on a 4 x 8-foot sheet of plywood, and with their tight curves and cramped space, they usually end up looking like a cat chasing its own tail.

In this book you'll find instructions for building an N scale layout that's a little smaller than that size, but—because of the smaller equipment—features a more open look. Such a layout can keep you entertained for years of building, detailing, and operating!

A significant advantage to building in N scale, even if you have enough space for an HO layout, is that the real world is a big place. Every time we model railroaders try to cram even a small part of it into even the largest room, we have to compromise. Towns that are supposedly miles apart are separated by a few feet, and we wish our 25-car trains were more like the prototype's 100-car trains.

If you want to capture the look of mainline railroading, consider taking an area large enough for a medium-size HO scale layout and then building that layout in N scale. Keep the separation between towns and scenic elements the same as they would have been in HO scale, changing only the track center-to-center spacing and perhaps the number of yard tracks. You'll find the resulting layout can be far more believable than the same plan built to HO scale. Suddenly those sharp HO curves look broad and majestic as a long train of beautifully detailed N scale cars roll past.

And speaking of N scale trains, don't let anyone ever tell you N scale doesn't run well. Anyone who holds that opinion hasn't seen the better N scale equipment on the market today. True

1-4

The relative size of N to the larger scales can be seen in these models of the popular Electro-Motive Division GP9 diesel. Shown from right to left are N, HO, S, O, and large scale (this one is 1:29) models.

enough, in N scale's early days there were many teething problems. Wheel flanges were too large, track appeared unrealistically heavy, detailing was crude, and locomotives ran too fast (or in some cases, didn't work at all). Today's N scale equipment is realistic and runs smoothly.

Ways to enjoy N scale railroading

There are as many ways to enjoy the hobby as there are participants. The only "rule" (and it's not really a rule, it's just common sense!) is to have fun and enjoy it.

While one person will find building models and then developing a layout to be an ideal way to spend his or her hobby time, another person may find a club setting to be the most rewarding way to enjoy the hobby.

Among the most common ways to enjoy N scale model railroading are building a home layout, building an Ntrak module, building models of locomotives, cars, and structures, and collecting some of the beautifully detailed N scale models that have been

made. Rather than concentrate on just one aspect of the hobby, most N scalers combine some or all of these activities. This book will concentrate on building and detailing a home layout.

The main goal of most beginning model railroaders is to build a realistic and functional layout. In a sense, model railroading is a combination of several hobbies and skills, brought together for the ultimate goal of creating a complete model railroad (**1-6**).

Before you jump headlong into building that first layout, be sure to avoid the three biggest pitfalls that cause beginners (and some advanced modelers) the most trouble:

1. Trying to do too much too fast
2. Refusing to try new materials or techniques
3. Failing to correct mistakes

The solution to pitfall No. 1 is easy: Start small. Even if you have a large basement to fill and can't wait to get started, make your first layout small and simple, and complete the entire sequence of construction up to and

including scenery and detailing. This will give you a chance to get a feel for every step of construction without getting bogged down in any one phase. An advantage of a small layout is that you'll often find that just about the time you get tired of one part of the process, it's time to move on to the next. It will also let you see which aspects of the hobby you enjoy the most.

When you start feeling comfortable with your abilities using one set of techniques, it's time to move on to step 2: Try different techniques. This may seem to be a contradiction. After all, once you get good at something, why change? As time goes on, you'll read model railroad magazines and books that highlight all sorts of interesting techniques from other hobbyists. Try them! If a new method of doing something doesn't work for you, it's no big deal. But if it does work, you may find the results better than you imagined.

And finally, don't ever be afraid to go back and change things to improve either the appearance of the layout or

1-5

A long Chesapeake & Ohio freight train winds its way through Afton, Va., on Bernard Kempinski's C&O module. N scale offers an ideal way to duplicate the way the landscape dominates a railroad. *Bernard Kempinski*

1-6

Locomotives, cars, structures, and scenic details (like the fences and people) all add up to a complete picture of life along the Santa Fe in the steam-to-diesel transition era on Verne Niner's Arizona Divide layout. *Verne Niner*

the operational reliability. Sure, the train sometimes derails on that turnout, but most of the time it makes it so why fix it? Believe me, if you take the time to get it working right, you'll be much happier in the long run. Not satisfied with how that mountain turned out? Rip it out and build it again. A mark of a truly excellent layout is that it stays fresh and advances with the hobby. Such railroads take on a life of their own over time, constantly evolving and improving as the builder's experience level increases and new materials and techniques become available.

Finding information

Throughout this book you'll find many techniques I've used in my own modeling. There is a veritable gold mine of information available to modelers today. Kalmbach Publishing, the publisher of this book, offers a wide range of books on virtually every aspect of model railroading. Three I highly recommend

you add to your library and read before getting too far into the construction of a layout are *How to Wire Your Model Railroad* by Andy Sperandeo, *Scenery for Model Railroaders* by Dave Frary, and *Track Planning for Realistic Operation* by John Armstrong. Although none of these are specific to N scale, the fundamental theories and techniques they cover apply to all scales, including N.

In addition to books, magazines are also a great source of inspiration and information. *Model Railroader* magazine, published by Kalmbach, is the oldest and largest magazine in the world devoted exclusively to scale model railroading. You'll find articles useful to N scalers in every issue. There are even two magazines dedicated solely to N scale, one titled *N Scale* and the other *N Scale Model Railroading*. Obviously, with their N scale focus they are must-reads for N scale modelers.

Another source of information is the Internet. Ten years ago it was hard to

imagine the impact the Internet would have on our daily lives. That impact has definitely been felt by the N scale hobby as well. You'll find all types of Web sites, message boards, and chat groups to suit your experience level and particular hobby interests. However, remember that although reading books and magazines or surfing the Web are great pastimes and excellent ways to enhance your knowledge of model railroading, at some point you have to put down the book (even this one!) or step away from the computer and actually build something.

This book is intended to help you grow from your first N scale car or locomotive to your first N scale layout. By the time you've built that first layout you'll find you've learned new skills, overcome challenges, discovered you have talent for one or more specific aspects of the hobby, and, best of all, had some fun in the process. Welcome aboard!

2-1

CHAPTER TWO

Planning your railroad

Lance Mindheim built his N scale layout following the real Monon railroad in Indiana. His model railroad captures the Monon's equipment, scenery, and operations in the 1950s. *Paul Dolkos*

New model railroaders, in their excitement and enthusiasm to do something, *anything,* sometimes rush headlong into building a layout without thinking things through. This isn't a disaster, since early mistakes can often be corrected, but it does explain why the resulting model railroad isn't always as enjoyable to build or operate as they first thought. Notice that this chapter is not called "track planning." There are plenty of books available on the mechanics of track planning and layout design. Instead, this chapter focuses more on the philosophy of planning the model railroad as a whole.

2-2

Bill Denton took advantage of the smaller size of N scale not to build a small layout, but to model New Lisbon, Wis., nearly to scale! The large scene allows realistic spacing among buildings, roads, and other elements. *Bill Denton*

Although it's tempting to dive right in and start building a model railroad, there's a real benefit to starting with a plan. Even a small model railroad represents a complex series of separate components and construction steps, and it doesn't make a lot of sense to build a complex anything—house, guided missile cruiser, model railroad—without thinking things through. The plan doesn't have to be overly detailed or involved, but it stands to reason that a railroad that has been carefully designed to fulfill a specific purpose will be far more satisfying than a layout that was thrown together in a haphazard manner.

There's no right or wrong way to design a model railroad, but no other process causes so many model railroaders to lose sleep or offers so much grist for the local hobby group bull session.

If you don't believe me, take your latest design down to the club or hobby shop or post it on an Internet discussion group. Model railroaders are naturally drawn to layout designs, and many will offer advice—some of it hard won. Be sure to listen and take notes, as some of those comments may be just what you're looking for.

Prototype, freelance, or both?

A key question you need to ask yourself before starting a design is what approach you want to take when planning and ultimately building and operating a layout. The answer will typically fall in one of three very broad categories: You'll determine yourself to be a prototype modeler, a freelancer, or something in the middle.

The lines of division aren't clear cut, and virtually all model railroads incor-

porate elements of at least two—and in many cases, all three—of these approaches. Which one you fall into will tell you a lot about what you expect from the hobby, and, in turn, where to focus your layout design efforts.

Prototype. In a way, all model railroaders follow prototype (real) railroading to some degree. This term has come to mean those who model a specific railroad or railroads as faithfully as possible. This includes not only the trains, but the buildings, bridges, towns, and even the recognizable scenic features of a specific place.

Prototype modelers choose a specific time period to model as well, and research everything about that era in detail. With the recent explosion of available products and the chance to model expansive scenery, N scale prototype modeling has grown in popular-

2-3

Mike Hurlburt chose a southern New England setting for his freelanced N scale Trap & Garnet Ridge. The T&GR interchanges with a prototype railroad, Conrail, which places the freelanced line in a specific time and place. *Keith Thompson*

ity in recent years. And, since N scale is relatively small, it's easier to duplicate the look of the landscape dominating the railroad (**2-1**) or to model an entire town (**2-2**).

Freelancing. I fall pretty hard on the prototype side of the model railroading fence, but I still appreciate modeling that doesn't closely follow a prototype railroad. If you like to buy anything in the shop you happen to see, or even if you just like to watch the trains run around continuously, you still have plenty of options. Freelancing means creating your own paint schemes, locomotive and freight car rosters, and even a complete railroad history—which can be quite elaborate. Many freelancers choose to place their imaginary railroads in a real world setting, usually by interchanging with recognizable prototype railroads (**2-3**). Other freelancers

don't bother trying to explain or justify the history and background of their railroads at all.

Prototype freelancing. There is a middle-of-the-road approach that combines the best of prototype modeling and freelancing. This approach, coined "prototype freelancing" by well-known model railroader and author Tony Koester, simply means taking the best of both worlds. You can invent your own railroad and set it in a real area of the country, or you can arrange for your fictional railroad to be a wholly owned subsidiary of a real railroad. By doing so, a lot of the "whats" that true freelancers have to answer about paint schemes, rosters, and such are already answered for you. You can mimic a prototype railroad's paint and lettering schemes, station and structure styles, and even use the real railroad's

operating schedules to develop your freelanced railroad's schedule. Truly effective prototype-freelanced railroads become quite "real" over time, and nothing seems out of place since questions are answered by looking to the prototype on which the layout is based.

There's another approach to prototype freelancing that can be a tremendous time and effort saver. It involves combining the equipment, some key structures, and other elements from an existing prototype in a way that best matches your interests and fits the space you have available. With this approach, your locomotives may all read BNSF or Pennsylvania, but the towns, track arrangements, and traffic patterns may not be precise duplicates of real places.

For example, at the town of Essex Junction on my old N scale layout, I

2-4

What are the "signature elements"—the items that must be modeled to capture the flavor of this prototype scene? This is Essex Junction, Vt., on the Central Vermont Railway. *Jim Shaughnessy*

2-5

Here's the author's model of the prototype Essex Junction scene. It features a scratchbuilt model of the train shed, a signature item that was certainly worth the extra effort. The other structures are kits that have been painted to resemble the prototype structures.

2-6

Jay Polk scratchbuilt this **N** scale model of Little Rock Union Station for his circa-1962 Missouri Pacific layout. The structure is a unique element based on a specific real landmark, and places the layout in a definite prototype locale. *Steve Crise*

scratchbuilt a rather elaborate model of the unique covered train shed that once stood in town. But when I started looking at all the other buildings that would have to be scratchbuilt if I wanted to create a true "prototype model" of the town, I knew I'd never get them all built. For that reason, I resorted to using kit structures that had the right look and overall appearance. A coat of paint and some weathering gave the resulting scene the look of the prototype even though most of the individual elements weren't exact prototype models (**2-4, 2-5**).

Do your homework

Now that you have defined your basic approach, you can start planning. If you want to model a prototype scene or railroad you'll obviously need to do some homework. Railroad historical societies, books, magazines, videos, and the Internet have made researching railroads easier than ever before.

Even if you're building a prototype-freelanced or entirely freelanced railroad you'll want to do some homework. Knowledge of a real railroad or railroads similar in geographic area, traffic base, or corporate culture can provide lots of great ideas to inspire your own

fictional creations. Enjoy the research and learn from it.

Keep two things in mind. First, research is a fascinating hobby in and of itself, but for our purposes it's a means to an end—that being the design of an interesting model railroad. Next, don't get so stuck in research that you never get anything built. Research will produce more questions that, in turn, result in more research. "Analysis paralysis" is the corporate-speak buzzword for this. Sure, it would be neat to know the exact style of grab iron applied to your chosen prototype's largest group of freight cars, or the exact format and style of waybills your railroad used. But is that information really necessary to get the layout design finalized so construction can commence? When you find yourself getting further and further in the weeds remember your goal, and ask yourself if you really need that knowledge to build a recognizable model.

Theory to practice

Once you've decided what you want to model, what your approach will be, and have done your homework, you're ready to begin trying to reduce parts of the real world to fit your space.

If you've read many layout design articles in *Model Railroader,* or any of John Armstrong's books on layout design (and if you haven't, you should!), you have come across John's term "givens and druthers." Simply put, "givens" are the must-have elements of a layout. The overall space is a given, as are things like prototype railroad, type of traffic, region of the country, or perhaps a signature structure.

"Druthers" are the "wanna haves" or "wouldn't it be neat if" elements. A large turntable with roundhouse, passenger terminal, or stockyard are examples of druthers. The trick is that you need to have all the givens but can be more selective with and prioritize the druthers. If five out of ten druthers make it to the final layout, the railroad will still be satisfying to you. This is where your research comes into play.

One technique you can use is to identify some of the "signature" elements of your prototype or prototype inspiration. Signature elements are features a knowledgeable viewer (and, thanks to your research, you'll be one of those!) would expect to see on a railroad based on a certain region of the country, era, or specific prototype. For example, the sight of a long train of

2-7

The Carolina Central is a simple oval layout built on a door, but thanks to the use of certain signature elements—a low pile trestle and rolling hills—even this basic layout captures the "look" of Carolina low-country without modeling a specific protooype location.

stock cars would be as out of place on a New England layout as a creamery would be in the middle of the Mojave Desert on a Southern Pacific-inspired layout. Unless you're modeling a specific prototype time and place, when forced to choose between a unique element or a signature element, the latter is almost always the better option. Use of these signature elements can be a far more powerful tool in creating a recognizable model of a prototype railroad (or making a freelanced railroad look more legitimate) than specifically duplicating track arrangements. Signature elements can transform a standard track plan into a model railroad with a recognizable theme (**2-6, 2-7**).

Start with a theme

A theme-based approach has worked well for me in designing layouts. My techniques in doing this have evolved (and will likely keep evolving) over time. It's not necessarily pretty, or even entirely logical, but it works for me and has provided me with somewhat satisfying results. If you're bound and determined to model Durango, Colo., as it appeared in 1928, or South Station in Boston circa 1945, by all means get out the prototype reference material and simply get to work. If, on the other hand, you have an inkling of what you want to model, and have a specific amount of space, time, or money within which you have to work, the theme approach might work for you.

You need a theme of some sort to end up with a layout that tells a cohesive story. The particular theme doesn't really matter. You can call it "Memories of Christmas Past" and feature a layout that has a Christmas tree permanently installed in the middle. Or you can set out to model part of Racine, Wis., in August 1953, researching and modeling every building, road, and tree in exacting detail. Both of these extreme examples are cohesive themes for a layout. But taking a detailed barnyard from the Racine layout and placing it in the middle of the Christmas tree layout would be just as confusing and distracting as plopping a snowman boxcar in the middle of a detailed prototype scene.

Design for the end user

All model railroads are built, viewed, and operated by humans. Therefore, it seems logical that layouts should be designed first and foremost with people in mind. Somewhat inexplicably, many model railroads end up being designed to accommodate the trains, some desired scenic elements, or to precisely duplicate every track found in a prototype scene—all without any regard for the people who have to not only build the layout but ultimately view and operate the fool thing.

Some of these factors are rather obvious things, like layout height and aisle width. Many features might not be so obvious, especially to a beginner. For example, it's easy to draw a track plan with hidden staging yards below the scenicked, visible level of a layout. This might look wonderful on paper, but have you really considered how you can build and maintain that hidden track? Have you ever tried to clean hidden track on a lower level? Do you have a plan for detecting where the trains are when you can't see them?

OVERPASS LOOP GRADES

Radius	GRADE	
	(1⅝") Minimum separation	(2") Normal separation
8"	3.0%	3.7%
9"	2.7%	3.3%
10"	2.4%	3.0%
11"	2.2%	2.7%
12"	2.0%	2.5%
14"	1.7%	2.1%
16"	1.5%	1.9%
18"	1.4%	1.7%

KEY PLANNING DATA

Proportion from prototype	1/160
Scale foot in actual inches	.075"=1 foot
Standard track gauge	.354"
Minimum track radius	7½"
Minimum track center-to-center separation	1¼"
Separation of tracks at overhead crossings	2"
Clearance from top of rail to underside of bridge or structure	1⅝"
Clearance from center of straight track to structures at side	⅝"

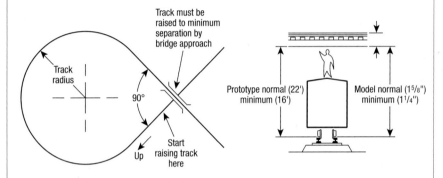

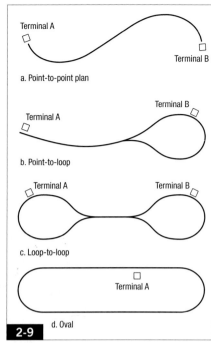

Layout types include point to point, point to loop, loop to loop, and oval.

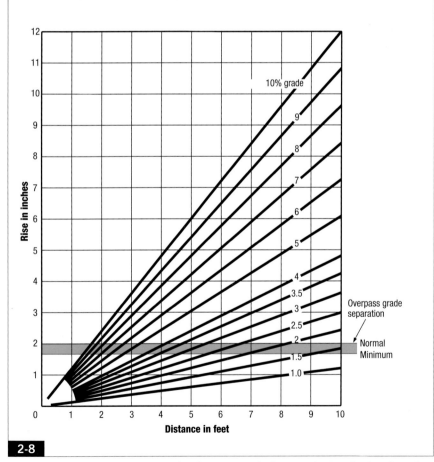

2-8

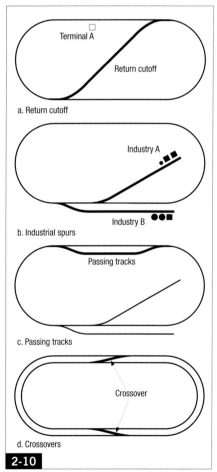

Return loops, spurs, sidings, and crossovers can all enhance operational interest.

Keep grades and overpass clearance in mind when designing a track plan. Grades above 2 percent begin to limit train length, but grades of 3 percent (and steeper) are possible with short trains, in industrial areas, and with slow-speed operations.

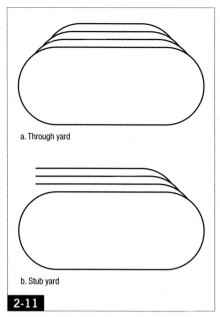

a. Through yard

b. Stub yard

2-11

Through yards offer more options, but stub yards have higher capacity.

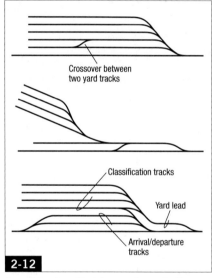

Crossover between two yard tracks

Classification tracks

Yard lead

Arrival/departure tracks

2-12

A yard lead avoids tying up the main line to work the yard.

Visit a model railroad—the scale doesn't matter—that has hidden track, and you'll notice how nervous people become when they're running trains they can't see. Providing them with a fancy detector panel and other devices can help, *if* the operators understand them. You will understand these things if you built them, but will your guests pick it up right away? Perhaps you'll find it's better to leave staging in the open. Besides, it's easier to build and you'll save on chiropractor bills by not having to climb under and around those hidden staging tracks.

Be realistic

By "realistic," I'm not talking about making the finished layout look like the real thing. Instead, be realistic about what you can accomplish. The old maxim is you can have something cheap, fast, or well-made, but you can only have two of the three. It's tempting—too tempting in fact—in the initial rush of enthusiasm to start construction of a layout that's too big, too complex, or too expensive to successfully "complete."

Many model railroaders fail to think this through, and in the rush to fill a newly acquired space with a layout find they've created a monstrosity that does nothing but gather dust, becoming a shelf full of unfinished projects, consuming time, effort, and money with little return on the investment. I've seen far too many railroads that are nothing more than sticks and some grandiose schemes and hand waving showing of "what will be."

Biting off too much is a danger that should be taken seriously. Think about all the structures that will need to be kit-built (or scratchbuilt) and the loco-motives and rolling stock that will be required to bring the layout to fruition. Then consider "real life"—remember, your time away from model railroading where you have soccer practice, school meetings, lawns to mow, decks to stain, and, yes, even golf to play and fish to catch. You may find later that you simply don't have the resources—and perhaps more importantly, the desire or time—to build a huge layout, even if you have the space for one.

So, if you're contemplating a large model railroad, take the time to think the project through. Be honest about the time, effort, and money you'll have to commit in order to see it through. If you think you can pull it off, go for it! However, don't hesitate to opt for a smaller layout. Building a small layout is always better than doing nothing at all. And an operational, well-scenicked small layout beats a basement full of lumber in my book.

Design for operation

Let's discuss two types of "operation" here. The first is reliable performance.

If the trains don't run well, you haven't really built a model railroad—you've built a big diorama. Your goal should be zero derailments, no stuttering, and no stalls. This means no quick taps with the ol' "0-5-0 switcher" (your hand) to get a stalled train moving when no one is looking.

Achieving this goal requires attention to detail in three areas: rolling stock, track, and electrical. But reliable operation really starts with design. Trying to cram too much track onto a layout or scene almost certainly leads to opera-tional issues. Complex trackwork result-ing in switching puzzles might look like wonderful challenges on paper, but may be virtually impossible for engines and cars to negotiate reliably.

The answer is simple. Every time you draw a line on a track plan, ask yourself what the purpose of that track will be. If you don't have a really good answer, leave it out. The result will be a railroad that not only looks better, it will perform better as well.

The second meaning of operation is in how well the layout simulates the movement of real trains. Do the trains have a purpose beyond visual entertain-ment? By considering the operating scheme before you start building the layout, you'll find the model railroad will be at least as enjoyable to operate as it was to construct.

Design for visual appeal

It's somewhat discouraging, or at least nerve-wracking, that after all the effort we take to lay flawless track, wire con-trol systems, and detail and weather locomotives and cars, the one thing most people will remember about our layout is the top $\frac{1}{8}$"—the finishing form, texture, and color we collectively refer to as "scenery." It's important to consider scenery when designing a layout.

As modelers go through the process of building a layout, many find they didn't leave enough room for scenic elements. Even the largest layouts are too small to allow for full-scale sce-nic effects, but luckily it's fairly easy to compress scenery so that it looks good even on a small layout. Your goal in planning and building scenery is to suggest the terrain being modeled,

2-13

Since N scale trains don't need a lot of room to function and the structures are small, modelers sometimes try to cram too much into an area for the scene to look right. The author found he initially went a little overboard with this town on the Androscoggin Central.

without trying to depict every hill, rock outcropping, and bush. Design significant scenic elements as you're planning the layout. That way when it comes time to build these scenic features, you'll know there will be enough room for everything.

Keep the prototype in mind when planning scenery. Mountain railroads most often follow river courses, meaning the mountains often tower above the tracks. On the plains, railroads don't have to contend with steep mountain grades but they have to cross rivers by passing over fairly deep ravines, often requiring significant bridges.

Also, consider the shape of the hills and the degree of slope. Many model railroads feature terrain that's too steep. This doesn't look natural. Although a tree-covered hillside can be steeper than a prototype since the foliage will lessen the apparent angle, keep the slopes gentle and the hilltops at a reasonable height.

Finally, be sure to include some scenic features below track level, such as rivers or dry washes. Not only do these add interest to the layout, they do wonders for getting rid of the "Ping-Pong table" look—a common problem in which track and structures appear as if they was simply plopped down on the ground.

Track planning

Before getting into the mechanics of layout planning, it's critical to keep in mind that even the best-conceived and most nicely scenicked model railroad isn't worth building if the trains won't work. Keep the grades reasonable and the curves broad. Figure **2-8** contains lots of key planning data on minimum radius, grades, curves, and clearances.

With all the thinking out the way, we're ready to put pencil to paper (or hand to mouse, if you're using a computer program) and see what we can actually fit in our space. This is often where the harsh reality of size and space limitations smack into the face of the wonderful theories outlined earlier, forcing us to make inevitable compromises. But it's a necessary part of the process.

What's the best method for actually drawing a track plan for your space? While there are a number of layout-design software programs on the market, I find my favorite layout drawing tools are an architect's scale rule, some graph paper, a few sharp pencils, and an N scale track template. If you plan to use a computer program, I caution you against using it too soon in the process. Some modelers get so engrossed in drawing track plans on their computers that they fail to start with some "free-form" sketches showing how a layout might fit the space.

Start by making a detailed scale drawing of your available space. Be sure to include all the obvious intrusions and obstructions and the necessary entrance and exit points: doors, windows, stairs, water heater, furnace, and workshop areas that tend to take valuable space away from our model railroads.

Also consider "vertical" obstructions. A few people commented on the narrow aisles and wide peninsula on one of my previous home layouts

2-14

Removing some buildings opens up the scene, makes it appear more natural, and allows some much-needed breathing room.

when the track plan appeared in *Model Railroader.* "If you narrowed the size of the peninsula, you could make the aisle wider." That may have seemed the case when looking at the two-dimensional track plan. What those folks couldn't see were the low-hanging ducts and water pipes that would have been a nuisance to me and a health hazard to my taller operators and guests. I built the peninsula in part to keep people from knocking into my plumbing!

The lesson here is to remember that although your plan is two-dimensional, the layout is being designed for a three-dimensional space.

When you finish your scale drawing, you'll realize two things: The space isn't as big as you'd like (everyone feels that way) and there seems to be a single obstruction that gets in the way of every wonderful plan you devise.

You have the choice of designing your own layout or copying (or modifying) a published plan from a book, magazine, or Web site. You can also "plan-bash"—that is, combine elements from one or more published plans to

2-15

The Ingersoll-Rand factory realistically towers over the trains on Michael Pennie's large N scale Penn Central layout. *Bernard Kempinski*

develop a new plan. This can be more troublesome that it may seem at first, since by copying a yard from plan A, a river crossing from B, and an industrial complex from C, you may inadver-

tently leave out a critical element or two. If you want to take the plan-bashing approach, I'd suggest showing your final plan to several experienced model railroaders. They may catch some criti-

2-16

Jeff Wilson modeled a container yard at a seaside port on a 2 x 4-foot Ntrak module. Container cranes and a ship are actually poster prints (enlarged from photos) glued to the backdrop. *Jeff Wilson*

cal omissions and save you a lot of time and trouble.

In looking for inspiration, don't ignore published plans for scales other than N. That 4 x 8-foot HO plan may look a little crowded, but could work well if adapted to N scale. Or that HO switching layout plan may provide the inspiration for an industrial district in your city. Best of all, your buildings will tower over the trains like they should!

In designing many layouts over the years, I have found that that the basic shape of the benchwork—the "footprint" of the layout—will usually suggest itself fairly early in the process. This is typically a shape that allows ease of access, proper placement of all the desired elements (yards, scenery features, and the like) and as long a mainline run as possible. I also tend to favor wider aisles and narrow bench-work where possible.

Whether you decide to create your own design, use a published plan, or come up with a combination of the two, there are a few track planning fundamentals you should know.

Schematics

Prototype trains run from one place to another and back again, stopping at various stations in between. A model railroad arranged in this manner is schematically a point-to-point system (**2-9**).

Adding a return loop, a track that allows the train to reverse its direction of travel, makes it a point-to-loop layout.

A return loop at both ends of the original point-to-point creates a loop-to-loop system. Finally, connecting the two ends of the original point-to-point together creates an a oval or circle, usually called a continuous-run schematic.

Continuous-run layouts provide for non-stop operation of trains. It's also traditionally the style most beginners want. Many times a novice will make a number of compromises on a plan in order to create a place to "just let the trains run." While there's nothing inherently wrong with that, consider that you can design a layout that takes up less space and provides greater operating interest if you forego the continu-

ous run in favor of a point-to-point or point-to-loop schematic.

You can also vary the oval schematic slightly by adding a return cutoff (**2-10**). The train can be turned on this track so it returns to town heading in the opposite direction.

It's important to remember that no matter how complex a layout seems, or how much track or routing options it has, all model railroads can be described in terms of at least one of these schematics. A good test for your track plan is to draw it in schematic form. Chances are if it's hard to figure out the schematic, the track plan itself may be too complicated to build, operate, or scenic, or for your operators to understand!

The schematic just shows the main tracks. You'll also want to consider other trackage to add operating interest and provide a place to store trains when they aren't actually running on the line.

Industrial spurs are a great way to improve even the simplest plan. Many published plans show industrial spurs,

2-17

The Chicago & North Western's Kenosha switcher works a siding at Berryville, Wis., on Keith Kohlmann's N scale Mini-Mod-U-Trak module. The group's standards specify two main tracks instead of the three tracks of Ntrak modules. *Keith Kohlmann*

but you may want to add additional spurs or rearrange them so your favorite industries will fit better.

If you want to run more than one train at a time you'll need to keep trains out of each others' way. On a single-track railroad the most efficient and common arrangement is a passing siding. A standard rule is one siding in each town, where the passing siding can also serve as a runaround track for switching facing-point spurs.

If you have a double-track mainline, the trains going in opposite directions never meet one another. But adding a pair of crossovers between the two tracks will allow a faster train to overtake a slower train traveling in the same direction.

Yard tracks. Most prototype yards are composed of smaller yards, each of which serves a particular function. But most yards are either stub-ended or through yards, as shown in **2-11**.

The stub yard is far more common on model railroads since it's less expensive to build and takes up less space than a double-ended or through yard. Figure **2-12** shows the makeup of a typical small yard. In this case the arrival/departure tracks are double-ended, allowing the yardmaster to use those tracks for trains going in either direction, depending on traffic. The classification tracks are the tracks on

which trains are made up or broken down.

Yard design and operation is a science in and of itself and we can't delve into it in detail here. For a great introduction to yard design, construction, and operations I highly recommend Andy Sperandeo's *Model Railroader's Guide to Freight Yards.*

Leave some breathing room

It's easy to give in to the temptation of cramming too many elements into a scene in N scale, with disappointing results. With N scale we often have the luxury of spreading things out a little bit. When I was designing the scenery, building placement, and roads for the Maine Central layout in chapter 9, it was easy for me to keep things spread out. I think that's because I had been building HO scale models for the previous two or three years. My eyes had grown accustomed to HO scale proportions, meaning I was subconsciously allowing more room between scenic elements. But I'm not immune to temptation, and it didn't take long for my eyes to readjust (**2-13**), and in those areas where I simply *had* to cram one more thing in place, I've gone back and removed things (**2-14**).

However, a nice feature of N scale is that you can have a large industry or structure that realistically dwarfs the

trains (**2-15**), something that is more difficult to do in larger scales.

Don't forget portable modules. A module can be designed to fit into a permanent home layout, or it can be combined with other modelers' modules to form temporary or semipermanent layouts. Modules following Ntrak standards (www.ntrak.org) are the most common, **2-16**, but some modular organizations have developed their own standards, **2-17**.

You'll notice my theory of model railroad design doesn't touch on track arrangements, layout shapes or types, or any of the mechanical details model railroaders often get hung up on. By thinking through the issues of usability, theme, practicality, operation (both types), and composition *before* you start drawing track plans, it will be far easier to produce a workable design you'll be happy with than if you start with nothing more than a blank pad and pencil.

Additional track planning tips

It's virtually impossible to model a prototype railroad foot-for-foot. And even if you could, it's not a good idea to do so. Let's face it: A great deal of prototype right-of-way is pretty uninteresting. Look for significant features on the prototype and model those elements, filling in the space between them with rather understated mainline running.

21

3-1

Benchwork

Benchwork is the foundation of your entire layout. With some simple techniques and basic tools you'll be able to construct a solid foundation for your railroad.

I've managed to build many model railroads, even though I consider my skills at working with wood to be minimal enough to guarantee being laughed out of any woodworkers' convention. What I do know about benchwork is that it must provide a solid foundation for the layout and be built in such a manner that it makes easier the steps of tracklaying, wiring, and scenery.

I've started enough model railroads in my lifetime to know a lot about building benchwork. More importantly, I've developed some pretty good ideas of what *not* to do. For instance, benchwork for my first layout was a piece of heavy scrap plywood (it must have been ¾") on a pair of sawhorses I found in the garage. This worked great for a while, but after a few months that seemingly solid piece of plywood developed a severe sag in the middle.

Over the years model railroaders have built benchwork from a number of materials, including aluminum, steel, foam, hollow-core doors, and, perhaps the most popular—wood. Each of these materials has advantages and disadvantages. The truth is that it doesn't much matter what material you use as long as it's strong enough to support its own weight over time.

Along with materials, there are many techniques of building benchwork. There is no one "right" way to do it, as several techniques might work well in a given situation.

Here are a few things you need to consider when planning and building benchwork for an N scale layout.

Portable, moveable, or permanent?

If you intend to stay in your current house until you are completely finished and done with your layout, then by all means nail or screw the benchwork to the walls, paint your backdrops in place, and use standard L-girder or open-grid benchwork made with dimensional lumber. Both methods are fast, and with today's inexpensive power miter saws, there is no difference in the time it takes to build open-grid or L-girder benchwork. Long ago, one oft-cited major advantage of L-girder was the ability to build a layout without having to make extremely accurate square cuts.

On the other hand, if you intend to move the layout at some point, you should build it with that in mind. Moveable is not the same as portable. A moveable layout is one intended to move once or twice during its existence, usually to a new residence. A portable layout is one designed and built to be frequently moved (Ntrak modules fit this category).

Rigidity: No matter what material you use for benchwork, it is critical that the entire structure be rigid enough to withstand handling without flexing. An example is a 4 x 8-foot beginner's layout we built when I was on the staff of *Model Railroader* magazine. It was constructed with a "box" of 1 x 3s forming the outer edges of the benchwork, with additional 1 x 3s laid flat—similar to a bed frame. Into this frame, we added layers of 1" or 2" inch foam insulation board. Our goal had been to build a very lightweight layout, and in that we succeeded. However, whenever we lifted the layout (no matter how light you make a 4 x 8 layout, the sheer bulk requires at least two people to maneuver it) the frame twisted, causing cork roadbed and scenery materials to separate from the foamboard surface.

Weight: This is not a common problem in North America, as we have a tendency to overbuild model railroads. However, it's still a good idea to keep the weight down as much as possible. Most model railroads have a lot of intricate detail and delicate scenery (such as water features, structures, and trees) that make the layout fairly fragile. The layout must be solid and heavy enough to protect these features while withstanding the occasional bump.

Scenery: If all we were doing was representing a section of the country with pancake-flat scenery, we could simply plop our track down on any solid, flat table and be done with it. Unfortunately for us, but fortunately for the appearance of our model railroads, the real world is not perfectly flat. Even in the prairies and desert the railroad sits above grade, with areas below the tracks providing for drainage. Including scenery elements below and above track level is critical to creating realistic scenery and should be considered before building the benchwork.

Lighting: I don't know how many times I've photographed a model railroad—either my own or someone else's —only to turn on the floodlights and think "Wow, that's what the railroad really looks like." I've known very few layouts

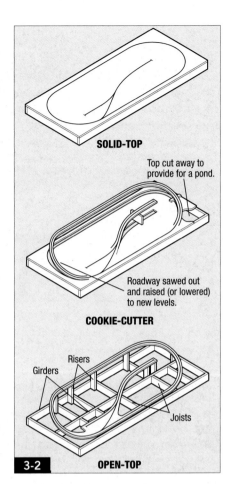

SOLID-TOP

Top cut away to provide for a pond.

COOKIE-CUTTER

Roadway sawed out and raised (or lowered) to new levels.

Girders
Risers
Joists

3-2 **OPEN-TOP**

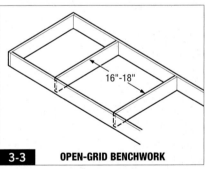

16"-18"

3-3 **OPEN-GRID BENCHWORK**

that are lit too brightly, but I have seen plenty where the owner and operators are really in the dark. It pays to consider lighting when building a layout. It may be also useful and easier, especially on portable or moveable layouts, to consider the lighting hardware as part of the benchwork.

Backdrops: Never underestimate the importance of a backdrop. Many modelers tend to categorize backdrops as "scenery," but the basic supporting structure and backdrop itself are really foundation/benchwork elements. In some cases it's efficient to combine backdrop supports with the lighting supports.

Hollow-core door layout table

When I built the Carolina Central, I used an ordinary 26" x 80" interior hollow-core door as the base for the layout. Check the seconds or damaged pile at a lumberyard or home improvement center, as a few dings won't impact its usefulness. Just make sure that the door is flat and the edges intact, since the edges give the door its structural strength.

I used folding-table legs to support the door. These make it much easier to build and operate the layout. I found the folding legs to be a bit low for comfortable viewing, so I extended the legs by slipping lengths of 1" electrical conduit over the legs and securing them with screws. Leveling bolts in the bottom of the legs keep the railroad on an even keel.

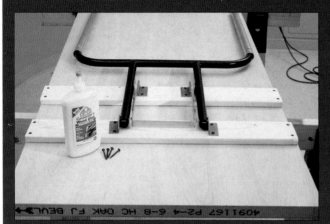

The position of the folding legs and braces determine the location of the 1 x 4 supports. Attach the legs to the 1 x 4s, not the door. For this layout I cut four 1 x 4s the width of the door, glued them in place with Liquid Nails, and screwed them at the edges.

To make the legs adjustable I added T-nuts to the bottom of each, hammering them into wood dowels as shown in the diagram.

Flip the table over, adjust the leveling bolts until the surface is sturdy and level, and the completed door table is ready for scenery and track.

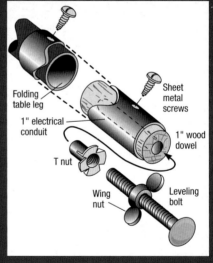

Folding table leg

1" electrical conduit

Sheet metal screws

1" wood dowel

T nut

Wing nut

Leveling bolt

Place a wing nut on the leveling bolt before screwing the bolt into the T-nut. The wing nut will lock the bolt in place.

Storage: When you're just starting in the hobby, it can be hard to imagine just how much "stuff" you can and will accumulate building even a small model railroad. A small layout has almost as much variety of individual items (screws of different sizes, tools, ground foam in several colors, etc.) as a large layout. The only difference is the small layout doesn't need as many of each individual item. Trying to find a place for all this stuff is enough to drive one out of the hobby. Many model railroads quickly become large shelves, especially in the early stages of construction. Try to avoid doing this, as it can negatively impact progress and sap your enthusiasm for the project.

Hollow-core doors

I have had outstanding results using hollow-core doors as layout bases. These doors are inexpensive, relatively light-weight, and dimensionally stable. You can support them on a table, on wood legs, or on folding "banquet table" legs. By placing 1 x 4s across the underside of the door you'll have a firm surface to secure the legs in place. The sidebar above shows how I built a basic hollow-core door layout table.

Hollow-core doors work well for layouts that may need to be moved out

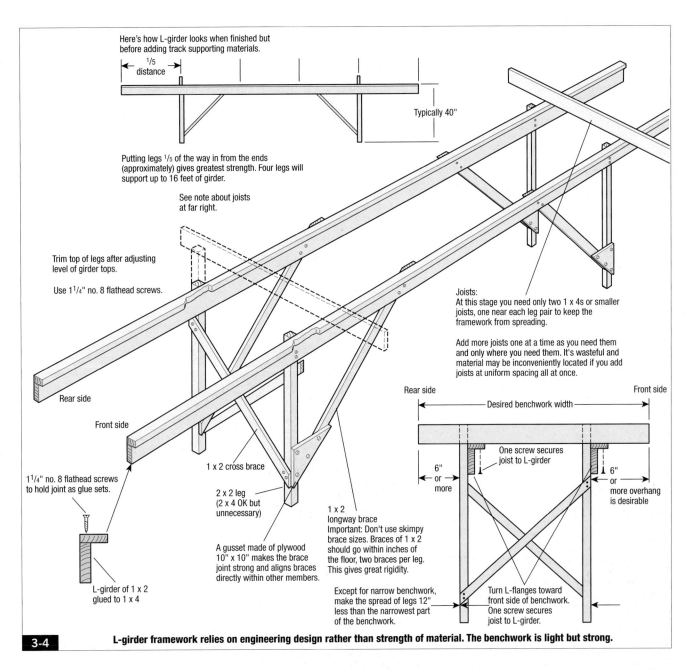

Here's how L-girder looks when finished but before adding track supporting materials.

1/5 distance

Typically 40"

Putting legs 1/5 of the way in from the ends (approximately) gives greatest strength. Four legs will support up to 16 feet of girder.

See note about joists at far right.

Trim top of legs after adjusting level of girder tops.

Use 1 1/4" no. 8 flathead screws.

Joists:
At this stage you need only two 1 x 4s or smaller joists, one near each leg pair to keep the framework from spreading.

Add more joists one at a time as you need them and only where you need them. It's wasteful and material may be inconveniently located if you add joists at uniform spacing all at once.

Rear side

Front side

Rear side

Front side

Desired benchwork width

One screw secures joist to L-girder

6" or more

6" or more overhang is desirable

1 1/4" no. 8 flathead screws to hold joint as glue sets.

1 x 2 cross brace

2 x 2 leg (2 x 4 OK but unnecessary)

1 x 2 longway brace
Important: Don't use skimpy brace sizes. Braces of 1 x 2 should go within inches of the floor, two braces per leg. This gives great rigidity.

A gusset made of plywood 10" x 10" makes the brace joint strong and aligns braces directly within other members.

L-girder of 1 x 2 glued to 1 x 4

Except for narrow benchwork, make the spread of legs 12" less than the narrowest part of the benchwork.

Turn L-flanges toward front side of benchwork. One screw secures joist to L-girder.

3-4   **L-girder framework relies on engineering design rather than strength of material. The benchwork is light but strong.**

of the way on a regular basis, or if you move fairly often. There are some limitations to hollow-core doors. Modifying the size of a door is difficult, as removing any of the edge pieces will compromise its strength and rigidity—two reasons for using it in the first place. Also, the sizes and shapes of available doors can be limited.

Conventional methods

Benchwork includes several components. The framework provides a solid mounting surface for the subroadbed—the (usually) wood supporting structure for the roadbed—as well as the scenery. The framework can be either an open

grid or a solid top, and you'll sometimes find it advantageous to combine both in one layout. For example, in areas where there are several tracks and/or structures, you'll want to have a large, flat surface. But when the track runs through open countryside, you'll find the open-grid method of framework construction more advantageous.

The most common methods of constructing model railroad benchwork are solid-wood-top, cookie-cutter, open-frame, or foam (3-2).

Solid-top construction offers several advantages. First, it requires the least amount of carpentry work. Ready-to-assemble workbench legs are available at

many home improvement centers, eliminating the need to construct legs.

In this method, the entire layout is built on a sheet of solid material, typically plywood, although a piece of rigid foam can be used. (Use the solid extruded type sold for building insulation, not the white beaded material like that used in coolers.) Track components can be laid out full-size on the table, so you know everything fits. It's also easy to make changes to the track plan before proceeding. The disadvantages of a solid-top layout become quickly apparent when you try to add scenery below track level, or if you want the track to climb up and over itself.

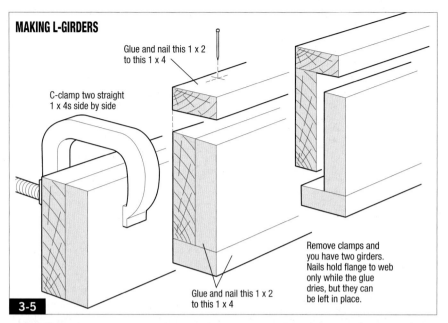

C-clamp two straight
1 x 4s side by side

Glue and nail this 1 x 2
to this 1 x 4

Remove clamps and
you have two girders.
Nails hold flange to web
only while the glue
dries, but they can
be left in place.

Glue and nail this 1 x 2
to this 1 x 4

3-5

Backdrop

Although backdrops are not technically benchwork, you'll want to think about them fairly early in your layout's construction. Otherwise, you may find yourself trying to install a backdrop on a scenicked layout, which can easily result in damaged scenery, structures, and other details.

A backdrop can be made from any smooth, nonporous surface. Over the years model railroaders have constructed backdrops from Masonite hardboard, styrene plastic, Upson board, drywall, and even posterboard. Of course, you could simply paint your walls blue.

What it's made from doesn't matter as much as what a backdrop can do to improve the appearance of any layout. The kitchen cabinets that were once visible just behind this dining room layout I built back in my apartment-dwelling days hardly contributed to the look of the Appalachian countryside I was trying to capture.

I fixed that by adding a backdrop made from inexpensive foam core. I painted it sky blue with some mountains and clouds. Even though the layout was unfinished, the visual improvement from just the backdrop was astounding.

Framework construction

The two most common methods of building model railroad framing are butt-joint, usually called "open-grid," and L-girder.

Open-grid benchwork consists of girders of 1 x 2 or larger lumber (1 x 4 is most common), which run lengthwise on the sides of the layout, and cross-pieces (joists), which reach from side to side and across the ends (**3-3**).

This method requires accurate, square cuts at the ends of each piece to produce strong joints and a square frame. The advent of relatively inexpensive power miter saws (commonly called "chop saws") has made it much easier and faster to get square cuts in benchwork lumber.

The L-girder method of framing was developed by Linn Westcott, the late editor of *Model Railroader*. The method derives its name from the shape of the main girders, which are inverted Ls, **3-4**.

The joists are secured through the flange of the L-girder from below, making it easy to move joists out of the way (of a turnout motor, for example) at any stage of construction. It is also easy to move, add, remove, and relocate a joist after the layout is complete without disturbing anything on top of the layout. In addition to simple alterations, L-girder benchwork requires less precise cutting and fitting than open-grid construction. Finally, since L-girder was designed especially to support model railroads, there is no wasted material. All the components contribute to the strength of the finished layout. An easy way to create the L-girders themselves is shown in **3-5**.

The subroadbed supports the roadbed and track, and is most often made with plywood. Once the subroadbed is cut out, it must be attached to the frame. It's a good idea to elevate the subroadbed above the grid, even if the track will be level (**3-6**). Raising the subroadbed above the joists or grid a couple of inches will make wiring and installing under-table switch machines much easier.

It may seem natural to locate benchwork legs at the corners, but for model railroads you'll often find it best to place the leg assemblies about one-fifth of the

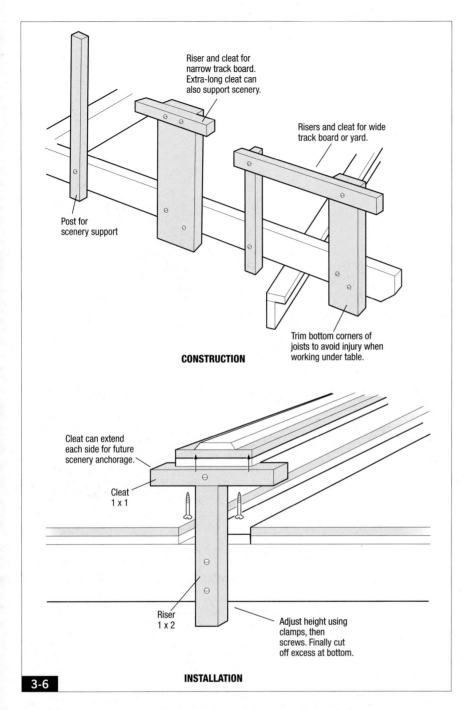

Riser and cleat for narrow track board. Extra-long cleat can also support scenery.

Risers and cleat for wide track board or yard.

Post for scenery support

Trim bottom corners of joists to avoid injury when working under table.

CONSTRUCTION

Cleat can extend each side for future scenery anchorage.

Cleat 1 x 1

Riser 1 x 2

Adjust height using clamps, then screws. Finally cut off excess at bottom.

INSTALLATION

3-6

way in from the ends of the girders. It also helps if you can set the legs in at least a foot from the viewing edge. This makes the legs less likely to catch the toes of your operators.

The best solution is to avoid legs altogether if possible. Narrow portions of the benchwork along the walls can often be supported using simple wood brackets.

Lightweight materials

The past decade or so has seen an increase in the number of layouts built using lightweight materials. This has long been true for portable layouts and modules, and has become common for modelers who live in apartments where the mess and noise of conventional materials and tools (such as plywood and power saws) make their use impractical.

Chief among materials used for lightweight layouts is extruded foam insulation board. This rigid material is available from building centers and lumber yards and comes in blue, pink, gray, or green, depending on the manu-

facturer. It can be glued to itself or to wood benchwork components with Liquid Nails for Crafts, latex contact cement, or Woodland Scenics Foam Tack Glue.

Foam insulation board comes in thicknesses from ½" to 3". It's easy to carve and shape, although it can take quite a bit of time and effort to get the smooth transitions needed for grades.

Woodland Scenics offers a line of foam components including precut roadbed material with different grades already pre-made. The company also makes the Mod-U-Rail benchwork system, with precut components that can be used for portable or permanent layouts.

Which method is best?

Open-grid benchwork is ideal for small layouts, especially if you have a power miter saw to ensure accurate cuts. This method provides an ideal base for solid-top or cookie-cutter construction, although I feel it's a case of overkill for layouts with lots of countryside. The basic construction of a series of boxes is remarkably rigid and works well for narrow layouts running along walls. The frame members make it easy to attach a shelf to the edge of the layout, although that same frame makes it difficult to achieve a curved, "flowing" look to the layout front.

I think most beginners would do best with L-girder benchwork and plywood subroadbed. These provide the best choices for ease of construction, strength, and versatility. Future changes to the layout are fairly simple to execute, and a large L-girder layout can be built in a weekend by one or two modelers armed with the appropriate tools.

Remember that there's no wrong answer. In fact, you'll find many larger railroads that combine both open-grid and L-girder construction.

Final thoughts

Benchwork may seem like a chore, but it's not. No other part of model railroading produces a visible result as quickly as benchwork. But take your time and do a good job. Since benchwork is literally the foundation of the entire layout, make sure that foundation is as sturdy as possible.

4-1

CHAPTER FOUR

Basics of track

Keith Kohlmann used etched brass joint bars from Alkem Scale Models to detail his track. This shot, on Keith's Chicago & North Western module, shows that N scale track can be quite realistic. *Keith Kohlmann*

Without reliable track, even the best-looking model railroad will become a dust collector. However, in our haste to make progress, we often use less care than we should when laying track. The result is a layout that doesn't run well, if at all. It pays big dividends to take the time to do it right the first time. Otherwise, you can find yourself ripping up completed scenery as well as track to fix the problems.

The appearance of track is also important. In many ways, track is the single largest model on any layout (4-1). Like anything else we want to model, it pays to know something about the prototype before attempting to build a model of it. You can see the components of a section of prototype track in 4-2.

Pay attention to the colors of the track as well as the ballast it's resting in. Keep in mind that track and roadbed in the steam era looked different than it does today. In the steam era, a wide bed of cinder fill was generally found beneath neatly edged rock ballast (4-3).

In those days when labor was plentiful and relatively cheap, section crews would carefully edge, or trim, the ballast edge and keep weeds and undergrowth away from the track.

There was a practical reason for maintaining a wide bed of cinder fill —hot cinders from steam locomotives would be less likely to start a brush fire if the undergrowth was kept away from the track.

As the steam era drew to a close, track maintenance became more mechanized, with a noticeable change in the ballast and coloration of the track. In the steam era, steam engines would drip oil from their side rods and running gear onto the outer edges of the track and ballast. Diesels didn't duplicate this. Instead, the weathering they produce is a noticeable streak down the center of the track.

Seldom-used tracks tend to have rail that's more rust colored, whereas rail that sees more traffic will have a dark brown to grimy black appearance.

An amazing variety of track products is available in N scale (4-4), making it possible to duplicate almost any prototype track arrangement. With a little care and some weathering and ballast, N scale track can look as good as that in larger scales. Large N scale layouts allow room for realistic sweeping curves and broad turnouts. Some N scale modelers handlay track to achieve truly stunning results.

Good trackwork starts with planning and the knowledge that there is a finite amount of track that can fit in

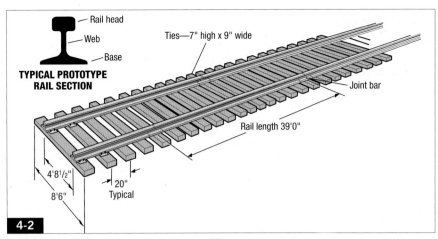

Here are the components and specifications for prototype track.

In the steam era, the ballast edge on most main lines was meticulously maintained. The cinder fill presented a stark contrast to the ballast.

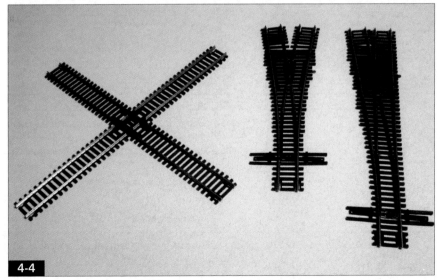

Many types of track sections are available, including crossings and turnouts of various angles.

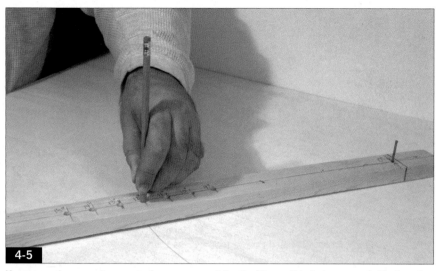

4-5

You can make a good compass from a scrap of 1 x 2 with a nail hole in one end. Mark and drill holes for each curve radius you plan to use. Tack the nail in place and draw the curve with a pencil.

4-6

A piece of flexible molding makes it easy to create transition spirals directly on the subroadbed. Lay the molding from the curve center line to the straight section and trace the line.

4-7

Remove the molding and you'll have a line indicating a smooth easement (transition) connecting the curved and tangent lines.

a space. It's tempting to force things "just a little" and make a curve a bit too sharp or add just one more turn-out. The result will often be a kink in the track and a place custom made for derailments. Avoid the temptation now and you'll be much happier with the end results.

Drawing curves

One of your first steps should be to determine your minimum radius. As a general rule, incorporate the broadest curves possible. Sharp curves—from 9" to 11" radius or so—will limit your ability to run long-wheelbase equipment such as six-axle diesel loco-motives, larger steam engines, and passenger cars, as well as auto racks, intermodal flats, and other long freight cars. This equipment can bind or derail on tight curves, and even if it does operate well, it won't look good because of excessive overhang.

Broad-radius curves are more reliable and look better. I'd recommend an absolute minimum of 11" radius for hidden track and industrial sidings and spurs, with no track sharper than 15" (preferably 18") radius for visible main-line track.

You also need to consider ease-ments, also called "transition spirals." An easement is a short stretch of curved track with a very broad radius between the tangent (straight) track and the constant curve. An easement, as the name implies, allows the train to ease into the curve, making it look and operate better.

Once you've completed your bench-work you're ready to draw the track center lines. Start with the curves. The easiest way to draw these is to use a length of wood with holes drilled every inch for various curve radii (**4-5**). A yardstick works very well for this and has the inches already marked.

Once the curves are drawn, you're ready to draw the easements between the curves and tangent track. Some modelers get pretty fancy figuring out the math to reduce prototype curve easements to N scale, but one of the best ways to get a nice smooth transi-tion curve is to use a piece of mold-ing trim or cork roadbed—something that's flexible enough to bend to your minimum radius.

Draw the center line for the tangent track, but don't connect it directly to the line for the curve. Instead, offset it slightly (about ¼" for most typical N scale curves).

Set a piece of flexible molding along the tangent line, bending it until it follows the curved sections. Hold it place (use a couple of small nails if necessary) and trace a line along the molding to connect the curved and tangent lines (**4-6**). The natural bend of the wood creates a workable transition spiral (**4-7**).

You can also transfer the above line to a piece of styrene or stiff cardstock and make a template that you can use on all the curves of a given radius. Making these in advance for your most common curves can save time.

Roadbed

Although you can lay track directly on your subroadbed, there are a number of reasons you'll want to consider using some type of roadbed to raise the track slightly above the "ground."

The first is appearance. Prototype track is elevated above the surrounding terrain to facilitate drainage, and modeling this increases realism. Roadbed has operational advantages as well. It provides a smooth base for track and can reduce the noise that trains make running on track attached directly to plywood or foam board subroadbed.

Several commercial roadbed products are available, with cork (from Midwest Products and others) the most common (**4-8**). Other roadbed includes AMI Instant Roadbed, Woodland Scenics Track-Bed, Hobby Innovations Vinylbed, and California Roadbed Co.'s Homabed.

Cork comes in perforated strips that must be peeled apart before installation. Homabed, made from Homasote (a fiber board commonly used for insulation) comes already split in half. Instant Roadbed, Vinylbed, and Track-Bed are one-piece products. Otherwise, the process for installing these products is similar.

Because the cork is divided into halves, it's easy to fasten along the track

4-8

Cork is the most widely available type of roadbed. It comes as a single piece but is split down the middle; peeling the halves apart reveals one beveled edge on each piece. Push pins hold the cork in place until the glue dries.

Peco Code 80   Peco Code 55   Micro Eng Code 55   Atlas Code 55   Atlas Code 80
4-9

N scale track options include, from left, Peco code 80 and code 55 (which has part of the rail imbedded in the ties), Micro-Engineering code 55, and Atlas code 55 and code 80.

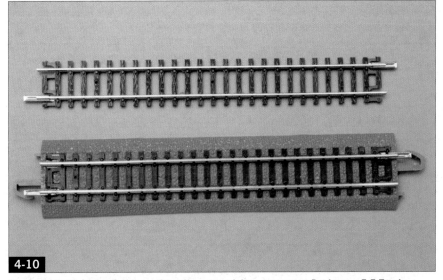
4-10

Sectional track is the first type of track most modelers encounter. Bachmann E-Z Track (bottom) comes with plastic roadbed, eliminating the need to ballast the completed track. Standard Atlas sectional track is shown at the top.

4-11

Place a length of flextrack in position on the roadbed, bending it to follow the desired curve. One rail will extend longer than the other. With a hobby knife, place a small notch on the longer rail even with the shorter rail.

4-12

Turn the flextrack over and use the knife to trim away the ties that will interfere with the cut.

Track sizes

One of the first mysteries of model railroad track is its "code." You'll often hear this term associated with track, and manufacturers offer their products in several codes. This is simply a way of indicating the height of the rail in thousandths of an inch. Thus code 40 track has rail .040" tall, code 55 rail is .055" tall, and code 80 is .080" tall. These are the three most common rail sizes in N scale (**4-9**).

Code 40 track is the closest to true scale size for N scale. Although flextrack is available in this size, ready-made code 40 turnouts are not available. Code 55 is a reasonable compromise. Although it's slightly large in scale, it still looks good and there's a wide variety of turnouts and other components available. Atlas really set the N scale modeling world on end a few years ago with the introduction of its large line of sectional track, turnouts, and flextrack in code 55. The track is relatively inexpensive, easy to work with, and looks great.

Code 80 was the standard rail height on most N scale track into the 1990s. Although durable, the rail is quite oversize compared to the real thing. This becomes quite noticeable in photographs.

Some N scale rolling stock and locomotives (especially older products) have wheels with deep flanges. These will not run on code 40 rail, and the flanges may bump the spike heads on code 55 track. Because of this (and for general appearance), many modelers equip all of their cars with low-profile wheels such as those offered by Micro-Trains, Atlas, InterMountain, and Fox Valley Models.

Most N scale diesels and steam locomotives made since the early 1990s will run fine on code 55 track, but for code 40 operation the flanges may have to be turned down—an operation not recommended for beginners.

Some experienced modelers choose to handlay track with individual ties and rail. One of the chief advantages of handlaid track is the ability to custom-build turnouts to fit specific needs and situations. Space doesn't allow a complete description of handlaying tech-

center line. With one-piece products you need to take extra care to make sure the roadbed is centered over the center line, especially through curves.

Instant Roadbed is a black, tacky material (uncured rubber). It comes in a roll and is designed to self-adhere to the subroadbed as well as the track. I've found that it does not adhere well to foamboard, but it does stick—very well—to plywood and to track.

Track-Bed is a soft foam material with beveled edges. It comes in long, continuous rolls.

Vinylbed comes in a variety of widths and heights, making it easy to build up a realistic subroadbed and roadbed profile. You can purchase pre-cut turnout sections of roadbed, but frankly I've never found it necessary.

Cork, Track-Bed, Homabed, and Vinylbed are all also available in large sheets. These are handy for multi-track areas and yards.

Which roadbed should you choose? There's really no best or worst choice. I usually opt for cork, since it's the most widely available product. I've used all of the other products either on my own layouts or those of friends, all with good results.

The key to any roadbed is to make sure the top surface is smooth and that it is firmly anchored to the subroadbed.

niques, and I'd advise against handlaid track on your first layout. However, once you become comfortable with other techniques, consider experimenting with handlaid track. You might find that handlaying would work for you on a future layout.

Sectional and flexible track

Most model railroaders get started with sectional track (**4-10**). This is the type of track included in train sets, and since it's easy to work with and a wide variety of components are available, it's a good choice for your first layout.

The quality of sectional track has improved greatly over the years. Newer types of sectional track come mounted atop plastic roadbed that gets the track (and more important, the locomotive gears) up and away from the carpet if you're setting up track on the floor. These sections also ensure positive mechanical and electrical contact.

Because the curves that come with sectional track are often sharp and toy-like, the most popular choice for N scale is flexible track. Flextrack comes in sections approximately 3' long (the exact length varies among brands). Spaces in the molded tie strip under the rails allow the track to be bent to virtually any radius. Flextrack allows you to achieve a more realistic appearance, since you aren't limited to the fixed-radius curves of sectional track.

Flextrack from different manufacturers has varying characteristics, so you may want to experiment a little to see which one you find easiest to work with. Atlas and Peco track sections are much easier to bend than those from Micro Engineering. However, once flexed, Micro Engineering track will hold the curve without being fastened in place; Atlas and Peco track will flex back to their natural position unless the track is secured. Many N scale modelers choose Micro Engineering track for visible areas and Atlas or Peco track for hidden track and staging yards.

A disadvantage of using flextrack, especially for beginners, is the need to cut the track to length. When you bend a section of flextrack, the rail ends will be uneven. This requires that the longer rail be cut to match the shorter one.

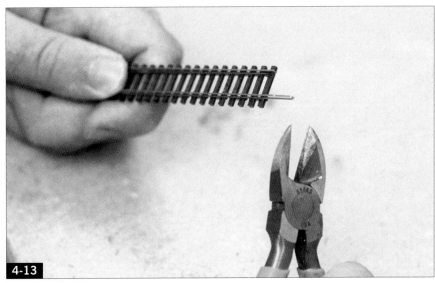

4-13

Cut the rail. Rail nippers work best for this. Nippers look like heavy wire cutters, but don't use them for anything except track! Wear safety goggles to protect your eyes.

4-14

Smooth the bottom, top, and web of the cut rails with a file. Slip a rail joiner in place and the track is ready to install.

Tracklaying tips

Here are a few things to keep in mind when laying the track on your layout:

First, the track must be in proper gauge at all times.

Secondly, rail ends must be matched perfectly, with no gaps, misalignments, or kinks.

Finally, straight track should merge into curves with some sort of transition curve or easement. This is simply a short length of track at each end of the constant-radius curve that has a broader radius. It allows for smooth flow of trains into curves without a sudden lurching that can cause operating problems.

Before laying the track, you need to consider how you'll be securing the track on the roadbed. There are three basic methods: gluing it down; nailing or tacking it in place; or using Instant Roadbed, with its built-in adhesive properties. Nailing track in place can cause lot of issues. Accidentally driving nails too far can buckle the ties and force the rails inward, causing operating problems. Bending a nail while driving it can break or dent a tie. Also, nail heads in the middle of ties don't look realistic. Because of this, I prefer to glue track in place. I explain how to do that in the in the Androscoggin Central project layout in Chapter 10.

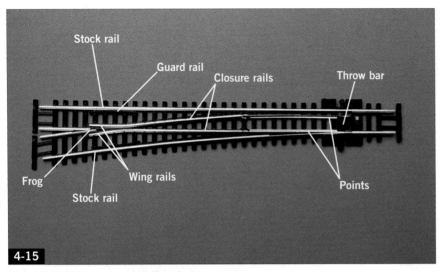

Stock rail
Guard rail
Closure rails
Throw bar
Frog
Wing rails
Stock rail
Points

4-15

Here are the components of an N scale turnout.

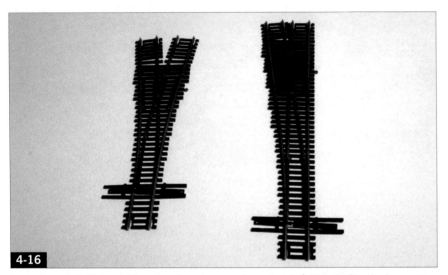

4-16

A wye turnout (left) has both routes diverging away from the straight path. Standard turnouts, like the left-hand model at right, have one route diverging from a straight route.

4-17

An abrasive track cleaner, such as a Bright Boy, works well for polishing the railheads.

Laying flextrack takes practice, but it's not difficult. The toughest part is cutting it to fit. You can see step-by-step how it's done in **4-11** through **4-14**.

Laying straight sections is pretty straightforward, but joining two pieces of flextrack on a curve can be tricky. Start by tacking one end in place with a brad or push pin, then lay the track into the curve. Bend the track to follow the curve, but leave the last 5" or so straight. Trim the rail ends flush and add the next section of flextrack. Solder the rail joints, allow the solder to cool, and file the joint smooth before bending the track through the rest of the curve.

Sight along the rail frequently to make sure there are no kinks or jogs between sections of rail. Joints between track sections should be seamless. If you can see a kink, you can be sure you'll have operational problems in those areas.

Turnouts

Turnouts, known on real railroads as "switches," are used to route a train from one track to another. Many separate components make up a turnout (**4-15**). Modelers generally use the term "turnout" instead of "switch" to avoid confusion with electrical switches. For example, if you tell someone to throw the "switch for the yard lead" it may be unclear if you're referring to the electrical switch or the track turnout. "Throw the turnout for the yard lead" makes it clear you're talking about track.

Turnouts present the biggest potential sources of track troubles. Trains can easily derail if a turnout isn't thrown completely, if the points don't press firmly against the stock rails, if the track is out of gauge at any point in the turnout, or if the frog is fouled.

Turnouts are identified by the direction of the diverging (curved) route—right or left—as well as by frog number. The frog number is a measure of how sharp the curved portion swings away from the main route. If the curved portion diverges one unit from the main route for every six units of length, it's a No. 6 turnout. A turnout in which both routes curve away from what would be the straight route, so

4-18

The CenterLine track-cleaning car guides a weighted metal roller wrapped with a cloth that's been dampened with track-cleaning fluid.

that it's shaped like the letter "Y," is, of course, called a "wye" (**4-16**).

The most popular brands of ready-made turnouts are Atlas, Peco, and Micro-Engineering. Bachmann and Kato also offer turnouts with their combination track/roadbed systems.

Most turnouts work well right out of the box, but it never hurts to do a little fine-tuning before installing them on a layout. I use a small file to gently file the ends of the points so they blend into the stock rails. This helps prevent the wheels from "picking" the points, the most common cause of derailments at turnouts. Also check the height of the point rail where it meets the stock rail. If the point is higher, file the point rail flush. Make sure the frog is free of burrs and obstructions. On plastic frogs, I use a sharp knife for this. With metal frogs, like those on Micro-Engineering turnouts, I use a small file. Finally, make sure all flangeways are clear of obstructions.

Cleaning track

Dirty track is a leading cause of poor operation in all scales, and can be a particular problem in N scale because of the small size and light weight of

4-19

The Aztec track cleaner uses a roller made of abrasive rubber material. It's frame is covered by an ordinary boxcar shell, so it blends in with other freight cars in trains.

the trains. The best solution is prevention. Having a ceiling in the layout room and keeping the room free of construction debris and other dust will help prevent track from getting dirty in the first place. Occasional track cleaning will still be necessary.

After construction, especially after ballasting and other scenery work, you'll need to really clean the surface of the rails. For this heavy cleaning I recommend a hard track cleaner, such as a Bright Boy, that you rub along

the top and inside surfaces of the rails (**4-17**). You can get track-cleaning cars from several sources. These are great since they clean the track as they move throughout the layout. Some modelers get a few track cleaning cars and operate them in trains like any other freight car (**4-18, 4-19**).

Another way to clean track is with a simple cotton cloth moistened with rubbing alcohol. Run this along the tops of the rails and you'll be shocked at the dirt this will pick up.

5-1

CHAPTER FIVE

Wiring and train control

Model railroads would be little more than static displays without wiring. It's wiring that allows us to capture the excitement and motion of real railroading. Here the author's son Matt uses a Digitrax Digital Command Control throttle to control a Maine Central diesel model.

Many beginning model railroaders believe you need some sort of special knowledge of electricity to wire a layout. In fact, you can wire a layout without knowing the first thing about electrical theory simply by following step-by-step instructions.

Wiring is really about getting your railroad to operate reliably and realistically (**5-1**). This chapter will cover the basics of wiring a layout, and if you're interested in learning more about model railroad wiring I highly recommend reading *Easy Model Railroad Wiring* by Andy Sperandeo. Andy offers a small smattering of electrical theory and chapter after chapter of practical knowledge gained through first-hand experience wiring simple and complex model railroads.

DC wiring

Wiring a layout to run a single train with traditional DC power is simple: Connect two wires from the variable DC output terminal on the back of the power pack (**5-2**) to the track as shown in **5-3** and **5-4**.

Terminal rail joiners make it easy to connect wires to the track (**5-5**). You can also solder wires to the rails. Terminal rail joiners are standard rail joiners with short lengths of feeder wire already soldered in place. Drill a hole in the layout, slip the rail joiner onto the track, and run the wire through the hole, connecting it with the wires from the power pack.

On small oval layouts you only need to connect one pair of wires to the track anywhere on the oval. For larger layouts it's a good idea to add feeder wires (**5-4**) at the opposite side of the layout. Without additional feeders, the train's speed can drop when it's far away from the wires and speed up as it gets closer.

Wiring a layout with turnouts can require special consideration. For example, Atlas and some Peco N scale turnouts are wired so both routes through the turnout are powered, regardless of the position of the points. Micro Engineering and some Peco turnouts are power-routing, meaning that the points route electrical power as well as the train. Layouts with power-routing turnouts must be wired with feeders at the point ends of the turnouts as shown in **5-4**.

What if you wire your layout to the power pack terminals and nothing happens? Or, even worse, the "short circuit" light comes on? Chances are very good

5-2

If you started with a train set that included a power pack, you'll likely want to replace that pack with a better model like this one from MRC.

you have a reversing section (a place where the train can reverse its direction of travel) that's causing the short. To wire reverse loops, you'll need to isolate the reversing section from the rest of the layout by adding insulated gaps in the rails and by wiring the track power for the reversing section through an electrical switch that will change the polarity while the train is in the reversing section. For specific instructions on wiring turnouts and reversing sections see *Easy Model Railroad Wiring*.

Wiring for two-train operation

If running one train is fun, then it stands to reason that running two trains at once must be twice as much fun. Although many N scale modelers now employ Digital Command Control (DCC), many still operate multiple trains using standard DC cab cab control (**5-6**).

To control more than one train with regular DC wiring, you must first divide the track into electrically isolated sections called "blocks." Figure **5-7** shows how dual-cab control works.

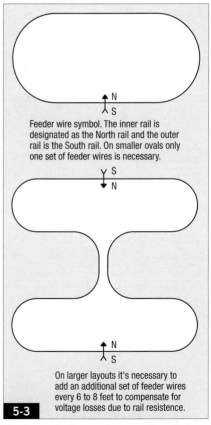

Feeder wire symbol. The inner rail is designated as the North rail and the outer rail is the South rail. On smaller ovals only one set of feeder wires is necessary.

5-3

On larger layouts it's necessary to add an additional set of feeder wires every 6 to 8 feet to compensate for voltage losses due to rail resistence.

The larger the layout, the more electrical feeder wires are needed.

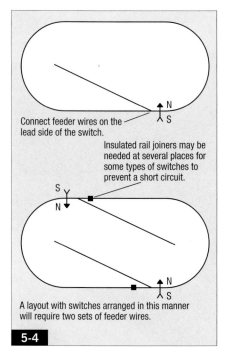

Connect feeder wires on the lead side of the switch.

Insulated rail joiners may be needed at several places for some types of switches to prevent a short circuit.

A layout with switches arranged in this manner will require two sets of feeder wires.

5-4

Multiple feeder wires are necessary on layouts with power-routing turnouts.

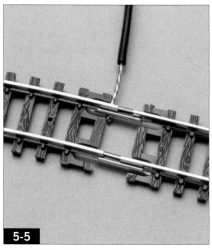

5-5

Terminal rail joiners make it easy to get electricity to the track without the need for soldering.

5-6

It's not necessary to have command control to operate multiple trains on the same layout. Standard DC control doesn't require installing decoders in the locomotives, but much more wiring (with many rotary or toggle switches) is necessary to to control multiple trains. This is Bill and Wayne Reid's famed Cumberland Valley layout. *Andy Sperandeo*

The track in **5-7** shows common-rail wiring, a type of cab control where one rail is electrically divided into separate blocks by gaps, and the other rail serves as the common electrical return for all blocks. Each divided rail of the two blocks shown in **5-7** is wired to the center terminal of a single-pole, double-throw (SPDT) center-off toggle switch. The lower terminal on each toggle switch is connected to the power pack on the left, which we'll call Cab A, while the upper terminal on each switch is connected to the pack on the right (Cab B). When the toggle switch is up, Cab A controls the block. When the toggle is down, Cab B has control of the block. Setting the switch in the center turns off all power to the block, which is useful for places where you want to park a locomotive or train.

Another variation on cab control is to have both rails gapped and use a double-pole, double-throw (DPDT) toggle switch. Although this requires a bit more wiring, it makes it easier to control reverse loops, wyes, and other complex trackwork.

The easiest way to gap rails is with plastic insulated rail joiners. These work well, but you need to know the gap locations before you lay the track.

Another method is to cut gaps with a cutoff disk in a motor tool (**5-8**). Be sure to wear eye protection when cutting rail (regardless of the cutting method). As the drawing shows, you can fill the resulting gap with a small piece of styrene secured with cyanoacrylate adhesive (CA). The plastic can be filed to shape after the glue dries and painted to match the rail.

Dual-cab operation is fine for smaller layouts, and can work well on larger layouts too. To use more than two cabs with standard DC, substitute rotary switches for toggle switches and add additional power packs.

One piece of advice: Try to keep the blocks as long as possible without detracting from your planned operating scheme. With several trains moving, it's easy to get so engrossed in throwing toggle switches that you never really watch the trains!

Wiring a layout for dual-cab control is pretty straightforward. Simply repeat the wiring diagram as shown on a control panel, mounting the toggle switches at the appropriate locations on the diagram. Mount the control panel on the front of the layout for easy access.

Walkaround control

Many of today's larger layouts are designed with long main lines that run on eye-level shelves along aisles. Each train passes through a scene only once before moving on to the next scene. To isolate operators and viewers from adjoining aisles or scenes, double-sided backdrops and multilevel layouts are becoming more common.

This creates a problem when it comes to train control. After all, what good is a centralized control panel with toggle switches and stationary power packs when operators can't see the entire railroad? How can they control their trains?

Because of this, most medium- to large-sized layouts have done away with centralized control in favor of walkaround throttles. Controls for switch machines and block power are mounted directly to the layout fascia, often directly below the turnout or block they control. Speed, direction, and braking controls are mounted in a small hand-held box with a cord that can be plugged into a throttle bus at one of several points on the layout. Typically, throttle jacks are located at each town. For multiple-cab control, color- or number-coded jacks and throttles can be used.

With walkaround control, switch machines aren't needed to control every turnout. The operators can throw turn-

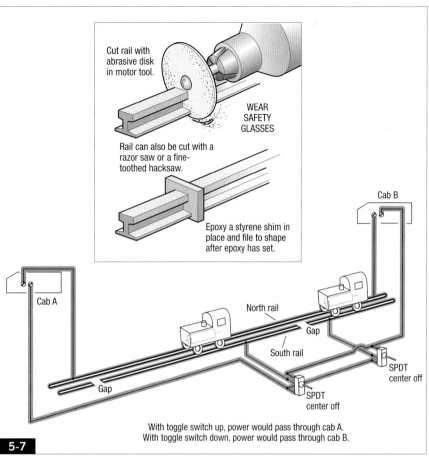

5-7

With cab control, power is routed from one of two power packs via toggle switches.

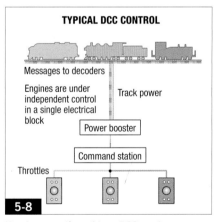

5-8

Here's an outline of how DCC works.

5-9

The top-of-the-line Digitrax Digital Command Control system, the Super Chief, allows many separate hand-held throttles to be plugged into the control bus at once.

outs manually, since they're following their trains.

But even if a walkaround cab-control system is ideal for many modelers, it still requires a tremendous amount of wiring, lots of toggle switches, and lots of time—most of it under the layout—connecting all those wires. Until about 20 years ago, that was the only option you had if you wanted to have a large operating railroad. However, since then, especially in the past 10 years,

command control has revolutionized model railroad control systems.

Digital Command Control

Since this hobby's early days, modelers have been trying to find ways to simulate the operation of real trains. Digital Command Control (DCC) allows us to do that, providing a means of independently controlling multiple trains on the same track without the need to switch block toggles on and off. I

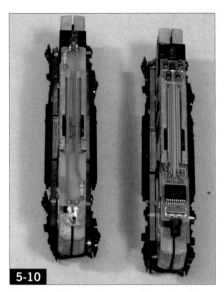

5-10

The only difference between these two Atlas GP38 chassis is the printed circuit board. The board on the locomotive at right has a factory-installed DCC decoder.

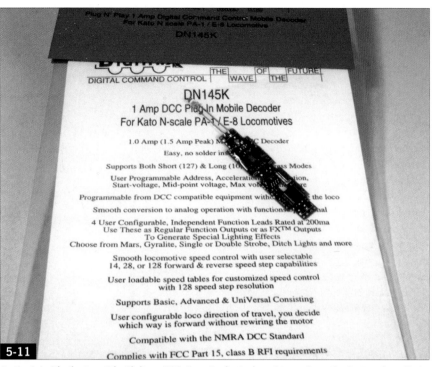

5-11

As the label indicates, this Digitrax DCC decoder is designed to replace the factory-installed circuit board in the Kato PA-1 diesel locomotive.

highly recommend DCC for anyone starting in the hobby.

With DCC, a constant voltage is applied to the rails, along with a series of digital signals (**5-8**). A decoder mounted inside each locomotive deciphers the signals and controls the motor, lights, and—on some locomotives—the sound.

Several companies make complete DCC systems, and some companies specialize in add-on or accessory equipment. Atlas and MRC each offer inexpensive entry-level DCC systems. These systems have some limitations, but they're a great way to get your feet wet without spending a lot of money. Other companies that specialize in DCC include Digitrax, Lenz, and North Coast Engineering. These companies each offer several systems geared toward a range of budgets and needs, ranging from simple systems for small layouts to extensive systems such as the Digitrax Super Chief (**5-9**) which can support the largest model railroads.

Radio throttles eliminate the need for operators to continually plug and unplug their throttles in jacks along the front of the layout. It also means operators won't get tangled in their throttle cords.

Specific systems and their capabilities change fairly rapidly, so I suggest looking at the various manufacturers'

Web sites and comparing systems at a hobby shop or large train show to see which system is the best choice for you.

To operate with command control, you need to install decoders in the locomotives. Some manufacturers now offer both standard and decoder-equipped versions of their locomotives (**5-10**). You can also buy decoders separately and add them to locomotives yourself. Many N scale decoders are designed to be swapped out for the model's printed-circuit (PC) board.

Luckily, with their split-frame design, most N scale diesel locomotives are remarkably easy to convert to DCC. Decoder manufacturers offer a number of drop-in decoders specifically designed to replace the factory-installed circuit boards (**5-11**).

If no drop-in decoder is available, or if you want to add DCC to an older model that doesn't have a full-length circuit board, you can hard-wire a standard decoder in place (**5-12**). The challenge with these decoders is finding enough room inside an N scale locomotive. Often the only solution is to file or mill away part of the frame. This can be tricky, especially for a beginner. A handy option is to use a frame that's already milled, such as those offered by

Aztec Manufacturing. I used an Aztec frame in converting the older Atlas GP7 in **5-13**.

The latest advances in N scale are sound decoders. These range in quality and as of this writing are relatively pricey, but the trend is obvious. Continued innovations in DCC technology will continue to revolutionize the way we control our trains.

Although command stations and throttles are not interchangeable among most DCC manufacturers, you can rest assured that your layout wiring and decoders will work with any DCC system. Many hobby shops stock DCC equipment, and several mail-order dealers specialize in DCC products.

Wiring tips

Regardless of whether you use a single power pack or go all out with DCC, there are a few general things you should keep in mind about wiring.

Wiring is much more than simply running wires from the track to the control system. The way the wires are routed is at least as important as the connections themselves. First of all, neatness counts: Label each wire at every connection point. At terminal strips, you can apply labels above or

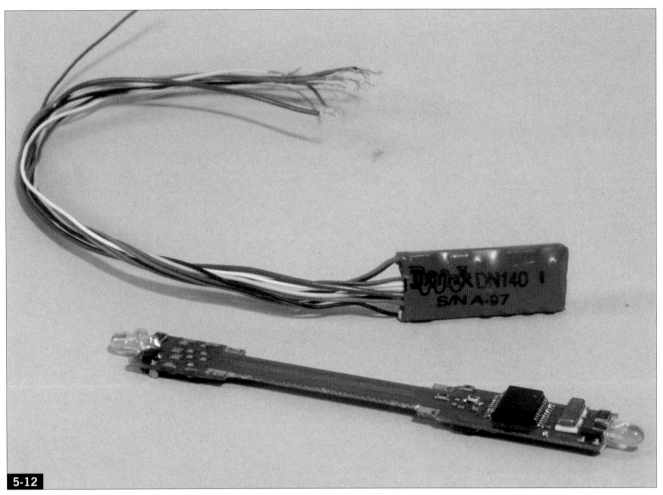

5-12

Here are the two most common types of N scale decoders. Drop-in decoders, such as the one at bottom, are designed for specific locomotives. Packet decoders (top) can be hard-wired into many different models.

below the screw terminal on the layout itself. Assign a letter to each terminal strip and a number to each post and record what each wire does.

Color-coding also helps. Settle on two colors of wire for track wiring (black and red, for instance), with other colors for switch machine wiring or layout lighting/ accessory wiring.

Don't run every wire in a perfectly straight line from one place to another. Instead, allow more wire length than you think you'll need. You'll be glad you did this if you ever need to splice into that wire in the future.

Good electrical connections are critical. There are several ways to get electricity from the wires into the rails. The most reliable method is by soldering the wires directly to the rails. Always use 60/40 rosin-core solder for any electrical work on your layout. Never use acid-core solder for electrical work, as the connections are likely to corrode over time.

5-13

These are both older Atlas GP7 models. The model in back is stock; the model in front has a milled frame to provide room for a packet decoder. Several companies provide this service (Aztec did this one). The precision-milled frame means the locomotive operates without binding—a risk if you try to mill the frame yourself.

6-1

CHAPTER SIX

Locomotives

The opportunity to operate steam and diesel locomotives alongside one another is one of the reasons the transition era is so popular among modelers. Here a Chesapeake & Ohio steamer meets up with the machine that will ultimately doom it to the scrap line. The steam locomotive is a brass import; the F7 diesels are by InterMountain Railway. *Bernard Kempinski*

The last 10 years have seen a boom in the variety and quality of N scale locomotives. Not only do these models accurately reflect their full-sized counterparts, the details, paint, and lettering equal or exceed those found in larger scales.

Perhaps the biggest improvements in N scale locomotives have been under the hood. As discussed in Chapter 5, DCC has really come of age in N scale. This means many locomotives now come with decoders installed or, at the very least, with simple decoder installation in mind.

We'll take a brief look at the variety of N scale locomotives available and discuss how to select models that are right for your railroad. Let's start with a brief look at the prototype.

Steam locomotives

Steam locomotives are classified by wheel arrangement using the Whyte system (**6-2**). The wheel arrangement tells a great deal about the use of the locomotive.

The first number in the classification denotes the number of wheels on the lead (also called pilot or pony) truck of the locomotive. The second number denotes the number of driving wheels (drivers), easily identified as the large wheels connected by rods on the side of the locomotive. The third number is the number of trailing wheels. Note that a locomotive need not have all three types of wheels. When it doesn't, the number "0" is substituted in the wheel arrangement. For example, a 2-8-0 has two lead wheels, eight drivers (four on each side) and no trailing wheels. Some larger locomotives have two sets of drivers under one boiler. These are articulated locomotives. A 4-6-6-4, which is also called a "Challenger," had four lead wheels, two sets of six drivers each, and four trailing wheels.

Most steam locomotive types were given nicknames, often a reflection of the railroad that first ran a locomotive of a particular type. Some wheel arrangements have two nicknames, again depending on the originating railroads. For example, a 4-8-4 is usually called a "Northern," except on the Nashville, Chattanooga & St. Louis, which prided itself as the "Dixie Line" and would have been hard pressed to call its 4-8-4s anything other than—you guessed it—"Dixies."

Steam locomotives of different railroads often shared some common

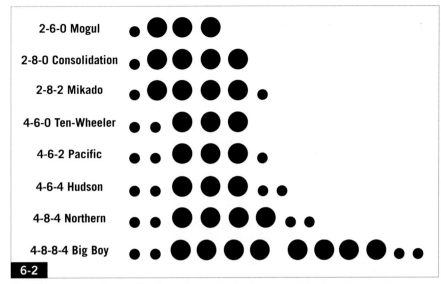

6-2

The Whyte system of classification relies on the total number of leading wheels, drivers, and trailing wheels to determine a steam locomotive's wheel arrangement (not all are shown).

6-3

The Central Vermont (top) and Santa Fe engines above are both 2-8-0 Consolidations. However, there is no mistaking one for the other. The CV engine burns coal, and the Santa Fe locomotive is an oil-burner; they also have different styles and sizes of stacks, domes, pilots, valve gear, headlights, bells, running boards, and other details.

6-4

Early streamlined freight diesels, such as the EMD FT, were referred to as "covered wagons."

6-5

Although the situation is starting to improve, for most steam locomotive prototypes imported brass models are really the only option. This is a brass model of a Santa Fe Northern with its stack extension raised. *Verne Niner*

6-6

The Kato USRA Heavy Mikado (2-8-2) ushered in the era of highly detailed N scale steamers that also run extremely well.

features, such driver arrangement and diameter. However, steam locomotives tended to be highly customized according to each railroad's needs and preferences. That means that although a Santa Fe 2-8-0 and a Central Vermont 2-8-0 (**6-3**) were both Consolidations, they were radically different machines.

The exception to this wide variance in steam locomotives came during World War I when the United States Railroad Administration (USRA) issued standard designs for a number of steam locomotives. While the locomotives that were ultimately delivered to the railroads had some minor variations, the USRA designs offer model manufacturers a group of locomotives that they can decorate with different road names and be quite authentic.

Diesel locomotives

The earliest diesel locomotives appeared on the scene in the 1920s, but it wasn't until the late 1930s that the "modern" diesel appeared. During World War II the tremendous demands placed on the railroads led to a number of railroads being authorized to purchase Electro-Motive's FT locomotive (**6-4**), which debuted in 1939.

The FT had enjoyed modest success before the war, but really came into its own during the war years, earning the monicker "the diesel that did it," with "it" in this case being the replacement of steam. It took a number of years but by the early 1950s it was obvious that the diesel would replace the steam locomotive. By 1959 the last steam engine had run its final miles in mainline revenue service on a Class 1 railroad in the United States.

In a diesel locomotive, a diesel engine drives an electric generator whose output powers truck-mounted electric motors. Unlike a steam locomotive's operating parts, most of which are visible externally, the mechanical parts of a diesel locomotive are hidden under the sheet-metal body. Diesel locomotive manufacturers offer standard models, which vary little from one railroad to another. This means that one railroad's GP40 will look virtually identical to other railroads' GP40s, with the possible exception of some minor details such as headlights, horns, and plows.

Early road freight diesels such as the EMD FT and Alco's FA had full-width carbodies that looked like

shorter versions of the manufacturers' six-axle passenger diesels like the E7 and the PA. Alco introduced its RS series (RS stood for "road switcher") in the 1940s, and diesel locomotives haven't looked the same since. The RS and its direct competitor, EMD's GP (which in the case of the locomotive stands for "General Purpose," commonly spelled "Geep" and pronounced "jeep") series, had long, narrow hoods with walkways on both sides and a short hood on the other side of a full-width cab. These road switchers didn't look as sleek as F units, but they offered better rearward visibility for switching and better engine access.

Modeling steam locomotives

Because of the wide variation in details and the railroad-specific nature of steam locomotives, comparatively few plastic N scale steam models have been made. And frankly, for many years the performance of even the best N scale steam models left a lot to be desired compared to diesel models.

Some decent older models are out there, including Bachmann's long-running Santa Fe 4-8-4, the Con-Cor series of engines based on the Kato

6-7

Athearn has entered the N scale steam locomotive market in a big way with locomotives like this 4-6-6-4 Challenger. It comes equipped with factory-installed DCC and sound.

4-6-4 mechanism, and a number of imported brass models, which have become better detailed but increasingly more expensive (**6-5**).

Models of USRA designs have wider appeal, and several good N scale models of USRA engines are available. Kato's USRA heavy Mikado (**6-6**) was perhaps the most-detailed plastic ready-to-run N scale steam locomotive when introduced in 1995.

Bachmann has offered a USRA 4-8-2 Mountain in both "light" and "heavy" versions as well as a USRA 2-6-6-2 articulated locomotive. And, although it's not a USRA design, Bachmann marketed a generic 2-8-0 model based in large part on an Illinois Central 2-8-0. The model successfully captures the look of Consolidations of several railroads.

More recently, Athearn, a longtime model railroad manufacturer but a relatively new player in the N scale marketplace, introduced both Union Pacific Challenger (**6-7**) and Big Boy locomotives with DCC and sound installed.

On the smaller end of the size spectrum, Life-Like (now owned by Walthers) released a beautifully detailed USRA 0-8-0 switcher (**6-8**). Although there are plenty of notable engines still

6-8

The Life-Like USRA 0-8-0 features fine detail and runs better than many imported brass models.

unavailable in N scale, the steam situation has improved and promises to get even better.

Modeling diesel locomotives

N scale modelers have a wide range of diesel models to choose from. Major manufacturers include Athearn, Atlas, Bachmann, Kato, and Life-Like (now by Walthers). Most N scale diesels have a one-piece plastic body mounted over a split-frame die-cast chassis that also provides weight for tractive effort.

The vast majority of N scale diesels on the market today reflect prototypes that were operating from the 1950s

through the mid-to-late 1960s. These include four-axle units such as EMD GP7s and GP9s and Alco RS-3s and RS-11s. A number of F units are also available. In the last few years, several examples of modern diesels have appeared on the market, including the Bachmann General Electric Dash-8, the Kato C44-9W, and the Atlas EMD SD60 and SD60M (**6-9**).

New models are continually being offered. This recent popularity of more modern motive power in no way reflects a declining interest in the older diesel locomotives. Those GP9s, F units, E units, PA-1s, and even rare

6-9

Although considered odd when introduced, almost all mainline freight locomotives today feature wide-nose "comfort" or "safety" cabs. This is a Kato N scale model of General Electric's Dash 9-44CW. Bernard Kempinski captured an SP version of this locomotive on his Tennessee Pass layout. *Bernard Kempinski*

6-10

Modeling the early diesel era allows capturing rare diesels like the Fairbanks-Morse C-Liner. Keith Kohlman photographed this Proto N (Walthers) locomotive decorated for the Milwaukee Road on his N scale module, as a 1951 Hudson waits at the crossing. *Keith Kohlmann*

prototypes like the Fairbanks-Morse C-Liner (**6-10**) continue to serve with pride on many N scale railroads.

In recent years, diesel detailing, once almost exclusively limited to HO and larger scales, has become quite popular among N scale modelers. A wide selection of detail parts is available, making it easy to duplicate not only the general type of diesel used by a prototype railroad, but all the details found on the real thing.

With a few hours, some detail parts, a new coat of paint, and some decals, you can transform an off-the-shelf model into a highly detailed model of the real thing (**6-11**).

This fairly recent interest in diesel detailing means that many manufacturers have enhanced their factory-painted locomotives more than ever before. For example, most top-end N scale locomotives now feature numbers in the number boards.

Don't get so hung up on the little details that you forget the easiest and fastest way to make any locomotive look super-detailed: weathering. A few washes with oil or acrylic paints, a little powdered chalk to tone down the trucks, fuel tanks, and walkways, and a factory-painted model will look super-detailed (**6-12**).

Selecting power for your layout

Ask yourself several questions when purchasing a new locomotive for your roster: Is it an appealing model? Does the model capture the overall flavor of the prototype? Does it fit your layout's theme? Is it available with a DCC decoder?

Back in Chapter 2 I discussed the importance of an overall theme in enhancing the realism of your layout. Ideally, a model should match a real locomotive found on your prototype during the time period you have selected to model. If you're freelancing, then you'll want to make sure the locomotive would have been a logical choice for your fictitious railroad.

6-11

Some simple additional details, such as a touch of paint on the dashboard and sunshades, etched windshield wipers, figures, and some homemade white "extra" flags, make this InterMountain F unit really stand out. *Verne Niner*

6-12

This Central Vermont RS-11 is a factory-painted Atlas model. Careful weathering with chalks and oil paints improved its realism without requiring any additional details.

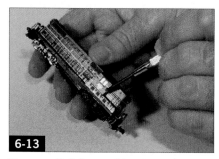

6-13

Use a small, flat screwdriver to gently pry the handrails from their mounting holes.

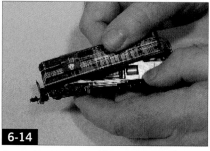

6-14

Squeezing the shell will disengage the latches that hold the body to the frame. Gently rock the shell from side to side while lifting it, and it will come right off the chassis.

Will the model operate well on your layout? Long locomotives with six-axle trucks will not operate reliably on sharp curves or turnouts. Make sure that any new locomotive will operate on your minimum-radius curves. Many manufacturers include minimum-radius information in their ads and packaging, and this information is standard in product reviews published in *Model Railroader* magazine.

Is the model offered in your favorite road name? Some models are available with multiple road numbers or unnumbered, making it easy for those who want to have a fleet of the same type of locomotives.

If a locomotive model isn't offered for your favorite railroad, you can paint and decal an undecorated model. N scale decals and dry transfers are offered by many manufacturers. Because locomotives are expensive, approach major alterations and complicated paint jobs after learning basic painting and weathering techniques on plastic structures and freight cars first.

Does the locomotive perform well? No matter how good a model locomotive looks, if it doesn't run well you'll never be happy with it. Acquiring an entire fleet of poor runners could easily frustrate you enough to give up model railroading entirely. Many hobby shops allow you to test-run models before buying them. Take note of how smoothly the model starts, how noisy it is, and how good the speed control is. Also check product reviews of the locomotive in the major magazines. Remember that a poor-running locomotive will never improve with age.

Maintenance

Most N scale locomotives don't need much in the way of maintenance. The biggest factor that inhibits performance of N scale trains is the same one that affects all scales—dirt. Regular cleaning of the track and locomotive wheels will keep this in control.

Clean locomotive wheels by dipping a cotton swab or a pipe cleaner into some ordinary rubbing alcohol and scrub the wheels. If the track is kept clean there's little need to clean locomotive wheels more than once or twice a year.

6-15

Here's the shell of an Atlas GP38 removed from its chassis and disassembled into its component parts.

You can also check for dirt and dust on the worm, worm gear, and universal joints inside the locomotive. It's impossible to describe how to disassemble every N scale locomotive—check the owner's manual or instruction sheet, which usually includes a diagram.

Most steam locomotive boilers are fastened to the frame by a screw hidden in the stack or under the steam dome. If no screws are visible from above, turn the model over and look directly below the smokestack between the cylinders. In addition to the screws there may be some tab-and-slot fasteners at the rear of the shell, typically on the rear wall of the cab. Remove the screws and then gently separate the shell from the chassis. Don't force anything! By noting the points of resistance you usually can determine the location of additional fasteners. After removing the boiler shell, you can determine the rest of the disassembly sequence by inspection.

Diesels are much more straightforward. The plastic shell is usually held in place by tab-and-slot joints along the bottom edges (**6-13** to **6-15**). Carefully remove the handrails from the holes with a flat screwdriver. Gently squeeze the body toward the center from both sides and lift the shell from the chassis.

Lubricate your locomotives with small amounts of plastic-compatible lubricants. The tip of a toothpick or a small piece of wire makes an ideal applicator. A little goes a long way, and over-lubricating a model will cause it to become a magnet for dust and dirt.

Some modelers develop a timetable for maintenance, such as lubricating each locomotive after every 100 hours of operation or every six months. I try to inspect each locomotive and clean and lubricate it once a year. Of course, if a locomotive is acting up, I'll pull it off the layout and take it to the workbench immediately. In most cases the problem turns out to be dirty wheels or dirty

commutators, or a loose connection on the PC board.

If a usually reliable locomotive is starting and stopping, even though the wheels and track are clean, your problem may be worn brushes. Motor brushes are exposed to more friction than any other part of a model locomotive, so it should come as no surprise that they need the most maintenance. Motor brushes are nothing more than small carbon slugs that provide a sliding electrical connection between the motor terminals and the commutator. The brushes are held in contact with the commutator with a small spring, and this assembly is held in place with a metal plunger called a brush cap. When the motor is running, the brush wears. The spring keeps the brush in contact with the commutator. When the brushes wear down and are no longer maintaining contact with the commutator the locomotive stutters and stalls. The solution is to replace the brushes.

7-1

Rolling stock and couplers

A wide variety of rolling stock is available in N scale, and the selection continues to expand on a regular basis.

Rolling stock—freight and passenger cars—is especially important to N scalers since we need so much of it. Some N scale club layouts regularly run 100- to 150-car trains, and home layouts that can accommodate 50- to 75-car trains are increasingly common. Even a 4 x 8-foot layout can gobble up cars at an astounding rate.

7-2

This plastic model of a single-sheathed 40-foot wood boxcar from Atlas is based on the large number of cars that were built during and after World War I following a standard USRA design.

There's been an explosion in available types of N scale freight cars in recent years. This has made it possible for modelers to acquire examples of almost every common type of freight car built for real railroads over the last 100 years. It's impossible in this one chapter to cover the thousands of N scale freight car models that have been made over the years. Instead, I'll provide you some general tips to help you select an appropriate mix of cars for your railroad and era. To accomplish this you need to start with a basic understanding of freight car history.

Freight car history

In general, wood cars are older, typically built into the 1920s. Freight cars with composite construction, such as single-sheathed wood boxcars on steel frames, were built primarily between World War I and World War II. The first steel cars built in quantity tended to be gondolas and hoppers (around the turn of the 20th century), since steel stood up well to the punishing service these cars experienced. By WWI virtually all hoppers and gondolas were steel, although material shortages—especially of sheet steel—meant composite gons and hoppers were built during both World Wars.

Wood and composite boxcars were common through the 1920s, but by the 1930s standardized designs made steel

7-3

The InterMountain N scale model of a 1937 AAR 40-foot steel boxcar represents a car that was common from the late 1930s to the early 1970s.

7-4

Fox Valley Models recently made a big splash in the N scale plastic freight car market with its assortment of modern 50-foot exterior-post boxcars like these Pullman Standard (PS) 5,344-cubic-foot-cars.

7-5

The 40-foot InterMountain ice-bunker reefer on the left and the Athearn mechanical refrigerator car on the right illustrate how refrigerator cars grew in size over the years. The Santa Fe car dates to the years before WWII and longer mechanical cars were common by the 1960s.

7-6

By the 1970s, 100-ton hopper cars were common. This is an Atlas model.

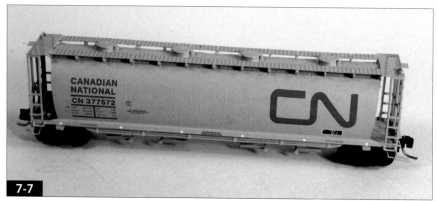

7-7

The Canadian government built large numbers of cylindrical covered hoppers for grain service starting in the early 1970s. The prototype cars were painted in colorful schemes as well as standard Canadian National and Canadian Pacific railroad colors. This is an InterMountain model.

boxcars such as the 1937 AAR boxcar (**7-3**) commonplace.

By the late 1960s those older 40-foot boxcars were wearing out or becoming obsolete. They were replaced with a variety of 50-foot exterior-post boxcars painted in a variety of paint schemes (**7-4**).

Refrigerator cars (**7-5**) are used to ship cargo that has to be kept cool. The earliest "reefers" were essentially heavily insulated boxcars. Bunkers on each end were accessed through roof hatches and filled with ice to keep the cargo cool.

Refrigerator cars were initially wood, some with very colorful "bill-board" schemes. In the 1920s and 30s steel reefers appeared, although they were still ice-cooled, and by the 1950s larger cars appeared, cooled by mechanical refrigeration. Ice-bunker cars were essentially obsolete by 1970.

Hopper cars (**7-6**), with their sloped interiors leading to a set of doors on the bottom of the car, carry bulk loads such as coal and gravel. At first these loads had to be weatherproof, until the 1930s when covered hoppers—with hatches in the roof—began to appear. At first covered hoppers were mainly

7-8

Tank cars come in a wide variety of sizes and types. The model at rear matches a prototype designed to carry kaolin clay slurry; the model in front represents a larger general-purpose car. Both are made by Atlas.

used for cement, lime, and sand. By the 1960s these cars were available in several variations, having become popular for grain, potash, salt, plastic pellets, and other commodities (**7-7**).

Like the covered hopper, the tank car (**7-8**) has undergone a tremendous evolution in recent years. Through the early diesel era, most tank cars were small—40 feet or less, with tanks from 8,000 to 12,000 gallons in capacity. The cars had steel frames, with bands holding the tanks to the frame. Today's tank cars are larger—up to 33,000 gallons—and frameless, with the tank itself providing the strength. Tank cars haul hundreds of products, including propane, ethanol, oil, gasoline, solvents, corn syrup, and vegetable oil. Cars with oil and gas company logos and names represent older cars—most modern tank cars wear nothing more than reporting marks, car numbers, and (if needed) hazardous-materials placards.

In the 1930s, when trucks were just starting to make inroads on the railroad's freight business, some railroads began experimenting with "piggyback" service—putting the truck trailer on a flatcar for the long haul portion of the

7-9

Modern container trains can trace their heritage to pioneering piggyback trains of the 1940s and '50s. Containers require specialized rolling stock, like this articulated five-unit well car from DeLuxe Innovations.

journey. The advantage to the shipper was obvious: The shipper only had to load the trailer once at his loading dock. This early TOFC (trailer on flat car) service has today evolved into the container traffic that accounts for the largest share of freight service on

railroads. Standardization allows a container to be loaded from a ship to a train to a truck chassis for a trip halfway around the world by land and sea.

Specialized container cars (**7-9**) with containers stacked two high (known as "well" or "double-stack" cars) snaking

7-10

Today's plastic caboose models, like these two from Atlas, are nicely detailed and rival the quality of brass imports of the 1980s and 1990s.

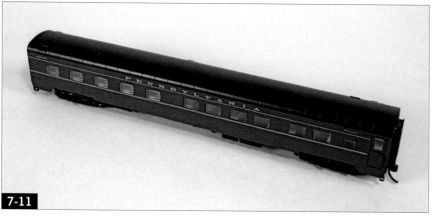

7-11

This Walthers 10-6 sleeping car is an example of the latest generation of N scale passenger cars available in ready-to-run in plastic. Although painted for the Pennsylvania RR, this car is also accurate for other railroads.

7-12

The Kato *Daylight* is one of a number of models of specific name trains that have been released in recent years. From the GS-4 steam locomotive to the observation car, the entire train is an accurate replica of the full-sized train.

their way through the landscape have become as much an iconic image of American railroading as the caboose was through the 1970s.

Speaking of cabooses, you'll have to work hard to justify one on the end of your trains if you're modeling the 1980s through today (**7-10**).

Developing a roster

Some modelers take a disciplined approach to selecting rolling stock, limiting their focus to a specific decade, year, or even month. Others take a broader approach. Study photos of your favorite railroad and you'll find it much easier to develop a realistic car fleet.

The most important factor is to select freight cars that fit your era. You'll also want to choose cars that reflect the traffic in the area you're modeling. A string of Chesapeake & Ohio hoppers would be out of place in the California desert. Likewise, a long string of yellow reefers would look odd on an Appalachian coal branch.

You should have more cars lettered for the railroad you model (your "home road") than any other single railroad. The percentage of home-road cars can vary—50 percent is a good rule of thumb through the early diesel era, with some railroads having a higher or lower percentage.

Finally, I believe the higher the percentage of "typical" cars, the larger the layout will appear. If every car is a colorful rolling billboard, every car becomes an attention getter. Operators will remember specific cars rather than seeing each car as another faceless cog in the railroad's transportation system. That's why a sea of nearly identical red boxcars or black hoppers, no matter what the road name, can make the car fleet, and therefore the whole railroad, appear larger.

Passenger cars

Passenger cars can be colorful and interesting and provide a nice diversion from freight cars. In the golden era of passenger rail travel, essentially through the 1950s, passenger trains of major railroads were a source of pride and intense competition. The first-class trains wore matching paint schemes and featured many luxuries.

Since they were the pride of the operating railroads, passenger trains were well maintained. They were assigned the newest and fastest locomotives on the railroad and given priority over every other train on the line. These trains carried coaches, sleeping cars, diners, lounge cars, baggage cars, and observation cars. Some carried mail and express shipments in specially decorated baggage-mail or Railway Post Office cars. Many were exclusive first-class trains, with no coaches.

On May 1, 1971, most of the long-distance passenger rail travel in the United States was turned over to the National Rail Passenger Corp., which is more commonly known as Amtrak. Amtrak was formed by an act of Congress to save intercity passenger service. Railroads had been abandoning passenger trains through the 1960s because of heavy operating losses. Amtrak operates trains today on selected routes across a number of the country's railroads.

Selecting passenger cars

If you want to ensure that your passenger equipment is completely authentic, you'll have to do some research. Most N scale passenger cars are based on a specific railroad's distinctive passenger equipment, but they're offered in a variety of popular paint schemes

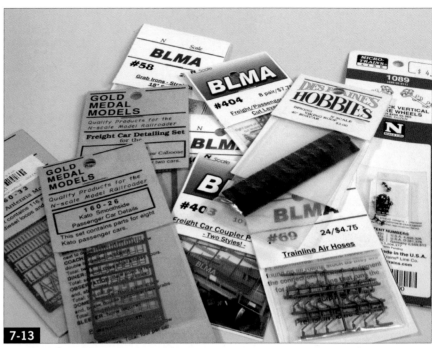

7-13

A tremendous variety of etched-metal and plastic detail parts are available. These parts make it easy to enhance the appearance of N scale rolling stock.

7-14

Compare the out-of-the-box Fox Valley MEC boxcar (rear) with a car painted in the same factory scheme (front) after it's had its paint faded and some basic weathering streaks applied with oil paints.

including railroads that may not have operated cars similar to them in appearance. Recently, manufacturers have begun offering a wider variety of ready-to-run passenger trains modeled after specific prototype cars (**7-11**).

As with freight cars, the earliest passenger cars were built of wood. Vestibules, closed walkways between adjoining cars, came into use in the 1880s. The first all-steel passenger cars were built in the early 1900s, and heavyweight (80- to 90-ton) cars were the standard from the early teens through the 1930s. The Chicago, Burlington & Quincy's *Zephyr* ushered in

the streamlined era in 1934. Welded stainless-steel components replaced the earlier riveted steel cars, reducing car weight to about 60 tons.

The newer stainless and lightweight painted smooth-side cars were also a perfect complement to the newfangled diesel locomotives then coming into vogue, and the streamlined era was born. The streamliners were beautiful trains, often painted in bold color schemes, and have always appealed to model railroaders. In the last several years, beautifully detailed models of specific name passenger trains have been released (**7-12**).

7-15

To create a faded look, start by spraying the car with light coat of Testors Dullcote, a clear flat lacquer.

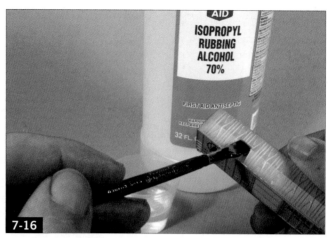

7-16

You can mist rubbing alcohol onto the model with a pump sprayer, but for N scale models I find it easier to control the alcohol by applying it with a brush.

7-17

The car on the right has had the area to the left of the door heavily faded. If you don't like the effect, simply recoat the car with Dullcote and start over. Washes with oil paints and some chalk (once the oil paint dries) will result in the effect seen in 7-19.

7-18

These two cars are factory-weathered Athearn models. Although not a bad starting point, they can be easily improved.

First-class passenger trains have always received the newest and best equipment, but railroads were reluctant to scrap older cars. Typically the older equipment was bumped into secondary mainline and branch-line service as newer equipment became available for name trains. Many wood passenger cars remained in service until after World War II, and heavyweight sleeping cars, many rebuilt with air conditioning added, operated in the Pullman fleet through the 1960s. Many heavyweight coaches, diners, and head-end cars served—especially on secondary trains—up to the Amtrak era.

Detailing and weathering

Read through some articles in the model railroad magazines and you may get the impression that every model on a layout has to be detailed to the nth degree. Nothing could be further from the truth. However, although many N scale cars look pretty good right out of the box, I'd encourage you to try to add some additional details to a few cars. A wide range of freight and passenger car detail parts is available, with the selection growing regularly (**7-13**).

Although adding individual details to a car is easy and fun, detailing a fleet of cars large enough to equip even a modest home layout can quickly become a daunting task. Perhaps the easiest way to increase the realism of any car fleet is to add weathering to the rolling stock.

Some N scale modelers I've met refuse to weather their cars and locomotives. I take the opposite approach, preferring to weather every car on the layout. (I do, however, sometimes press cars into service before weathering them—with the intent that they will eventually get some weathering!)

Weathering helps convey a sense of texture and size that's just not there with fresh out-of-the box N scale rolling stock. The difference between an unweathered and weathered car is truly startling (**7-14**).

I start by fading the paint using a trick popularized by a number of the top weathering artists in model railroading. By spraying the factory painted car with Testor's Dullcote, then brushing on ordinary rubbing alcohol, the body color will fade. For a more faded look, apply additional coats of alcohol (**7-15** to **7-17**).

Recently, some model railroad manufacturers have begun offering "factory-weathered" cars. These are standard models with a light overspray of road dust or grime that, considering the mass production methods used, aren't too bad (**7-18**). I prefer to think of these as nice starting points for additional weathering effects (**7-19**).

If the difference is that significant for one car, imagine what weathering the entire car fleet will do for the realism of your entire layout! You can even perfect your techniques to duplicate the exact weathering pattern found on a prototype car (**7-20**).

Specific weathering techniques are beyond the scope of this book. To do the subject justice really requires a volume of its own. For more on weathering check out Jeff Wilson's book, *Painting and Weathering Railroad Models* (published by Kalmbach). For specific techniques on weathering cars I also recommend Scott Mason's DVDs *Weathering Freight Cars, Volume I* and *Volume II,* available through his Web site, www.scottymason.com.

Trucks and wheels

The trucks are the assemblies that hold the wheels under each end of a freight car. Into the 1960s most freight car trucks were solid-bearing. These trucks had journal boxes over each axle end, and they required frequent lubrication. Covers on each journal box opened to allow crews to inspect and oil the journals.

Modern trucks all feature roller bearings, distinctive in the rotating end caps on each axle. These trucks require much less maintenance and are more free-rolling than solid-bearing trucks. Micro-Trains and InterMountain offer a variety of replacement trucks to match many prototype styles.

A wheelset is the combination of two wheels mounted on an axle. Most N scale freight cars come with one-piece molded plastic wheelsets. Some have deep flanges; others have shallow

7-19

Toning the roof down with burnt umber and raw sienna oil paints, adding an accumulation of simulated dirt and crud to the door tracks, and adding some rain streaks down the sides have added interest to this factory-weathered model.

7-20

The author used a prototype photo he found on the internet to model this faded and fairly heavily rusted blue and white USLX Evans boxcar.

flanges. As long as your track is laid properly, shallow-flange wheelsets work fine, and they look much better than deep-flange wheels.

Some freight car models now come equipped with metal wheels, and metal replacement wheels are available from Fox Valley Models, InterMountain, and Kadee. Many modelers prefer metal wheels as they add weight to a car and lower its center of gravity. Metal wheels also stay cleaner than plastic wheels, and they help keep track cleaner, as friction between the wheels and track effectively polishes both surfaces.

Couplers

Two types of couplers, each with numerous variations, have been used by

prototype railroads in North America: the link-and-pin and the knuckle.

Link-and-pin couplers were used from the earliest railroads through the end of the 19th century. Cars were coupled together by hand, often requiring a trainman to stand between two cars (one moving and one stationary) to guide the link into the slot and drop the pin in place. Obviously, this was very dangerous, and many railroaders lost fingers or were killed when the process didn't work.

In the 1880s railroads started converting to the knuckle-type automatic coupler invented by Eli Janney, the same basic design in use today. Opening the coupler knuckle allows couplers to mate automatically. Uncoupling is

7-21

Rapido couplers were once standard equipment on most N scale locomotives and cars (with the notable exception of Micro-Trains products).

7-22

Most N scale cars intended for the hobby market now come equipped with some form of knuckle coupler, either the popular Micro-Trains Magne-Matic (left, on a Fox Valley car) or the Accumate, used by Athearn (right) and Atlas.

7-23

Magnetic uncoupling ramps can be permanent (above), intended for mounting under track on a layout, or portable (below), designed to be placed between the rails above the ties.

accomplished using a lever that disengages the knuckle pin. The crew member does this while standing beside the car instead of between cars.

Coupling and uncoupling N scale cars together is not dangerous, but it can be frustrating. Several couplers are on the market, including the Rapido, the Micro-Trains Magne-Matic automatic knuckle coupler, the Accumate knuckle coupler (found on some ready-to-run cars and engines, primarily Atlas), and several one-piece knuckle couplers such as those made by Inter-Mountain and Red Caboose.

Rapido couplers (**7-21**) are rare on new equipment today, but were the standard coupler on models into the 1990s. Rapido couplers are simple in design and operation. The couplers have a pointed front edge and are free to pivot up and down. When two couplers meet, one coupler rides up over the other and falls into place, coupling the cars together. Their main problems are appearance—they're oversize and look nothing like real couplers—and uncoupling. Separating cars can be challenging—a small pick can be used to lift up one coupler.

Solid-knuckle couplers, like those made by InterMountain and Red Caboose, look much more like prototype couplers. They couple automatically when two cars are pushed together. They can be uncoupled by lifting one end of one car up. Many modelers, even those who prefer operating couplers for their freight cars and locomotives, use these solid knuckle couplers for passenger cars and multi-unit locomotive sets. Since these couplers aren't automatic, they're less likely to accidentally uncouple than any other style of coupler. They also permit locomotives to be coupled closer together.

The Micro-Trains Magne-Matic and Accurail Accumate (used by Atlas) are automatic knuckle couplers. These couplers are also used by other N scale manufacturers as well (InterMountain, for example, has included both Atlas and Micro-Trains couplers on its N scale cars and engines). These look and operate more like the real thing, and are the couplers of choice for most serious N scalers (**7-22**).

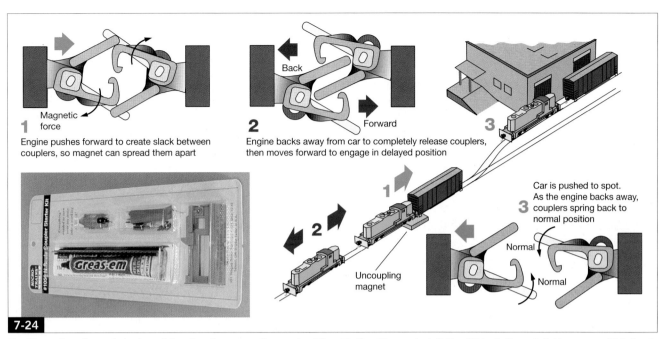

1 Magnetic force

Engine pushes forward to create slack between couplers, so magnet can spread them apart

2 Back / Forward

Engine backs away from car to completely release couplers, then moves forward to engage in delayed position

3 Car is pushed to spot. As the engine backs away, couplers spring back to normal position

Normal / Normal

Uncoupling magnet

7-24

The illustration above shows how delayed-action uncoupling works. Micro-Trains offers an installation kit including a height gauge and lubricant.

The coupler, including the shank, has two horizontal layers: The knuckle is attached to the top half and the remainder of the coupler head is attached to the lower half. The couplers open and close with a scissors action. When two cars are pushed together, the knuckles spread apart and then close together to engage.

The real magic of these couplers is the way they uncouple. A small steel wire, called an uncoupling pin or trip pin, hangs below each coupler. A magnetic uncoupling ramp (**7-23**) pulls apart the pins on adjoining couplers when the couplers are located above the ramp. You can see how these couplers work in **7-24**.

Accumate couplers work the same as Magne-Matic couplers. Coupling the two types of couplers isn't an issue, but getting the two brands to uncouple over a magnet can be a little tricky. Manual uncoupling (with a sharp stick, like a barbecue skewer) works well and doesn't require planning locations for uncoupling ramps. Just slip the stick between the coupler knuckles and twist.

Micro-Trains offers a vast line of couplers, trucks, wheels, and other accessories. If you have a locomotive or car that doesn't have knuckle couplers, odds are good that Micro-Trains makes a conversion kit (**7-25**) specifically designed for it.

7-25

Micro-Trains offers several coupler conversion kits for older cars and locomotives.

7-26

For reliable operation, all couplers should be the same height. You can check your rolling stock using the Micro-Trains No. 1055 height gauge. Make sure the uncoupling pins are also at the correct height above the rail or they could catch on something and cause a derailment.

If you have a lot of conversions to do, I recommend that you obtain one of Micro-Trains' Coupler Starter Kits. These kits include one each of several types of couplers, some dry lubricant, and a test gauge (**7-26**).

Installing these couplers is fairly straightforward: Just follow the instructions and use the recommended coupler. Properly installed, magnetic couplers will add greatly to your railroad's appearance and operation.

8-1

CHAPTER EIGHT

Structures: Models that don't roll

Structures say a great deal about the region and era of any model railroad. In urban areas the structures *are* the scenery. Bernard Kempinski built this Chase Marine Terminal scene by combining components from a number of commercial kits. *Bernard Kempinski*

If you're new to the hobby, it's likely that the first N scale model you'll construct will be a building (structure) kit. Structures provide important visual clues about your railroad's purpose, making them critical components of a model railroad.

8-2

Before Walthers released an N scale steel mill, Bernard Kempinski used components from several Walthers HO scale steel mill kits, with N scale detail parts added, to make a blast furnace that loomed over the trains—just like the prototype. *Bernard Kempinski*

8-3

Since the Model Power Baldwin Locomotive Works kit wasn't large enough to look right for his Kingsbury Branch layout, Bill Denton combined several kits to create the E.B. Millar & Co. building. *Bill Denton*

8-4

When Jim Kelly needed a fertilizer plant for his Ntrak module, he couldn't find any commercial kits with the proper appearance. He used readily available kit components for the various tanks and scratchbuilt the rest of the complex. The result is unique, and it looks appropriate for the area Jim models. *Jim Forbes*

8-5

The Walthers Superior Paper Company is an easy-to-assemble plastic kit that looks large enough to require rail service yet is compact enough to serve as the centerpiece of a small layout.

Building structure kits is a great way to get started in model building for several reasons. Their familiar components are less intimidating than those found in a rolling stock kit, especially for a beginning modeler. Structure kits are also large enough, even in N scale, to be easy to work with.

A large number of N scale buildings are offered in assembled form. If kit assembly and modification doesn't appeal to you, these might meet your needs, especially if you paint and weather them to make them unique.

Let's start by exploring the different types of buildings on and around the railroad and the various types of kits that are available in N scale.

Four ways to a structure

There are four basic ways to approach buildings for your layout. You can purchase the buildings already assembled; you can put together a kit "stock" (following the instructions); you can "kitbash" (modify a kit or combine two or more kits); and finally, you can "scratchbuild" a structure using various raw materials and components.

When building a stock kit, you'll find repainting the model with flat model paint, or at least adding a flat clear coat like Testors Dullcote, enhances the appearance.

Building a kit as the manufacturer intends means your model will look identical to those on hundreds, if not thousands, of other layouts. For generic buildings this is fine, but often you'll find it's worth the time and effort to kitbash or stratchbuild a unique structure.

When looking at structure kits, you can sometimes look past the scale on the box label. In larger scales, like HO, large industrial structure kits are often compressed. This means that some large HO kits are really closer to N

This Alkem Scale Models model of a coaling tower is an example of a mixed-media structure kit. The intricate steelwork of the prototype has been reproduced in brass, while the body of the tower is made from acrylic plastic. The dump house and other wood components of the prototype are reproduced by laser-cut sheet wood.

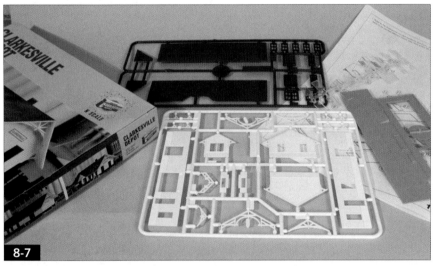

Lay out the parts of the kit. Review the instructions and familiarize yourself with the assembly sequence. You must also decide if you should paint any components prior to assembly.

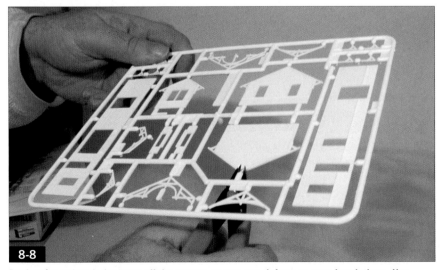

Don't twist or break the parts off the sprues, as you can deform or even break them. Use nippers to remove the parts.

scale in overall size. If the kit has relatively few windows and doors, it's relatively straightforward to add some N scale details and create a truly massive structure for your layout (8-2).

Kitbashing may sound like the desperate act of a frustrated modeler, but the term really implies a much gentler approach. The late Art Curren, a well-known modeler who popularized the process, preferred to describe it as "kit-mingling," since you're really altering, combining, and rearranging components into a finished model. No matter what it's called, the basic process is the same: Start with one or several kits, often from different manufacturers, and combine the various components or pieces to create a unique building that might not look anything like any of the original kits that went into it. You can also combine several samples of the same kit to make a building that's larger than the original (8-3).

If you just can't find an appropriate kit or components to match a building that you need to have on the layout, you'll have to resort to scratchbuilding. As the name implies, that means taking raw materials and building a model without the benefit of a kit. This may seem scary at first, but the process is often easier than it sounds. Despite N scale's small size, scratchbuilding in the scale is fairly easy, since many of the details that have to be included for a model to look "right" in the larger

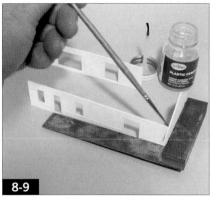

8-9

Use a square to keep the walls aligned, and apply a small dab of liquid plastic cement to the top of the corner with a small brush. Capillary action pulls the cement into the joint, bonding the parts together. Allow the cement to dry before touching or moving the model. It will set fairly quickly.

scales really aren't required on an N scale building. And a scratchbuilt building (8-4) can easily become the centerpiece of a scene, giving the layout a unique look.

Kit assembly tips

Visit a well-stocked N scale hobby shop and you'll be overwhelmed by the variety of structure kits. Years ago, many N scale structures were overly compressed, just like their larger-scale counterparts. Happily for us modelers, many of today's N scale industrial and business structure kits are large enough to look like they actually require rail service. (8-5).

The most common materials for N scale structures are plastic, wood, resin, and etched brass. Some are classified as mixed-media kits—these combine multiple dissimilar materials in a single kit (8-6A, 8-6B).

Don't let the material the kit is made from scare you; choose buildings that look appealing and interesting.

Regardless of the style of kit, start by reviewing the instructions and looking at the parts to familiarize yourself with the various subassemblies and components. Study the relationship of the various parts. Most plastic kits have parts identified by a letter or code on the inside edge of the part or on the sprue. On laser-cut wood kits, the parts are identified either on the wood or in a template in the instructions.

Building a Laser-Cut Wood Store

I've always had a thing for old country stores with their assortment of advertisements and wide selection of merchandise. Many of the ones I've visited and see in pictures stocked everything a "mile wide and an inch deep." So when American Model Builders released its N scale laser-cut kit for the Corydon General Store and Post Office, I couldn't resist building one. Who knows—perhaps we can add a little character to this building as we construct it.

1. After pressing together the tabs of two of the walls, apply a small amount of yellow glue to the inside corner with a toothpick. A machinist's square keeps the corner aligned.

2. After the walls dry, carefully pry up some of the clapboards with a hobby knife. You can age it by carefully slicing off some of the bottom edges of the clapboards. Go slowly—it's very easy to overdo this. The side and rear walls look more distressed than the front.

3. Add the roof, which also includes interlocked tabs, and paint the building with a thin coat of Polly Scale Aged White.

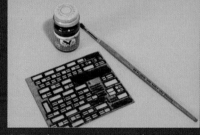

4. The windows, doors, and trim have peel-and-stick backing that secures the parts in place without glue. Paint the trim pieces and windows before removing them from the large wood sheet. The windows and doors are Polly Scale Maine Central Pine Green.

5. The signs (from Microscale and Blair Line) and the weathered siding give this model a great deal of character.

8-10

The Dubois Store from Branchline Trains is just one of the many N scale laser-cut wood structure kits on the market today.

8-11

American Model Builders (AMB) was one of the first manufacturers to produce laser-cut wood structure kits. The company offers an extensive range of large and small prototype-based railroad and non-railroad structures.

8-12

This country barn from Sylvan Scale Models is an easily assembled resin kit. The key to successful resin kits is painting them in a way that brings out all the molded detail.

It's often best to paint structure parts before starting assembly. Windows, doors, and trim are often a contrasting color. You could assemble the building and carefully paint the trim, but it's usually a lot easier to paint these parts while they are separate. Weathering can also be easier to apply before everything is assembled.

Do you plan to install an interior or lighting in your building? Consider how you can install them and, in the case of lights, how you can reach them later to replace bulbs.

Consider ways of giving structures some character. Opening a door, adding a patched section of roofing, or placing some special signs on an exterior wall are all neat ideas that will be easier to do when planned ahead of time.

Plastic kits

Start by removing the parts from the box and spreading them out (**8-7**). When you're ready to begin, be sure to cut parts from sprues as close to the part as you can. Twisting parts off the sprue can break or distort them. Instead, cut large pieces with nippers like those made by Xuron (**8-8**). For small parts use fine sprue nippers like those from Micro-Mark or Inter-Mountain. A good set of nippers will remove the part from the sprue without leaving a nub; it's still a good idea to file or sand the surfaces smooth so stray material doesn't interfere with the fit later.

It's important to keep wall joints square (**8-9**). A small steel square works well to hold mating walls in alignment while applying cement. By applying liquid plastic cement to a joint with a brush, capillary action will pull the cement into the joint, producing a firm bond. Be careful your fingers don't touch the cement—the plastic will be soft enough to take a fingerprint, marring the model. It's easiest to assemble walls as two "Ls," each made up of one side and one end. Once these set completely, glue the two L-shaped sections together, one joint at a time.

Wood structure kits

For many years, wooden structure kits were the province of the experienced

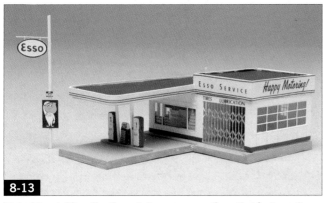

8-13

Etched-brass kits offer fine window cross sections that just aren't possible with other materials. This service station is produced by Showcase Miniatures.

8-14

This Model Power brick factory comes already assembled (left). The details are fine, but the building had too much of a plastic look. Washes of light gray paint (applied wet and then wiped off with a rag) added mortar lines, and weathering powders toned down the rest of the structure. The result (right) fits in with more complex and expensive structures with very little effort.

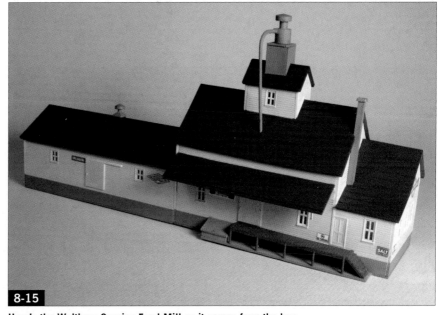

8-15

Here's the Walthers Sunrise Feed Mill as it comes from the box.

modeler. They required a lot of cutting and fitting of strip and sheet wood. Today, most wood structure kits feature laser-cut walls and details. The precise cutting action of the laser takes all the guesswork out of assembly. American Model Builders (8-11) was one of the first manufacturers of N scale laser-cut structure kits. But the same techniques for assembly and painting apply to any laser-cut kit from any manufacturer.

To assemble a laser-cut kit (see the sidebar on page 63) you'll need many of the same tools required for a plastic kit, although you can forego the sprue cutters and the liquid styrene cement. To assemble a wood kit, use yellow carpenter's glue or a high-quality white glue. Place a small amount of glue onto a small piece of scrap material and then use a toothpick to apply the glue to the model. As with plastic kits, a small machinist's square works well to keep joints square. In most laser kits the walls and roof components are notched, making it difficult to assemble the model incorrectly. It does, however, make kitbashing these structures a little more difficult.

Some laser-cut kits use peel-and-stick adhesive backing, especially for smaller details like trim and windows. The instructions explain how to assemble the components—be sure to follow them carefully and keep the parts aligned before pressing them together, as it's extremely difficult to pry these pieces apart without damaging them.

Just as with plastic kits, it's a good idea to paint the window trim and doors before installing them, especially if you plan to have trim in a contrasting color.

Two other materials, resin and etched brass, have become more popular for structures in the past few years and their use will likely continue to grow. Some resin buildings are one-piece castings with doors, windows, and details cast in place; others are similar to plastic and wood kits, with individual walls and roof components. The Sylvan Scale Models kit in 8-12 is an example.

The two most important things to remember about resin kits are to make sure the parts are clean (otherwise paint won't adhere to the resin) and use cyanoacrylate adhesive (CA) to assemble the kit, as plastic cements won't bond resin.

Etched-brass kits, like the Showcase Miniatures gas station (8-13), are among the most finely detailed N scale structures.

They are also more expensive than plastic or wood kits. Some of the more elaborate brass kits require applying several layers to a single base piece. This is helpful when the kit is for a Victorian house, for example, that calls for several colors of trim. Most brass kits require bending along etched guidelines. In some cases, reverse folds are required. It's always a good idea to carefully read the kit instructions when dealing with brass kits.

Factory-assembled structures

Pre-assembled buildings in N scale are nothing new, but most early examples

8-16

After spraying the model with Dullcote and then brushing on rubbing alcohol, the model might not look good. Don't panic!

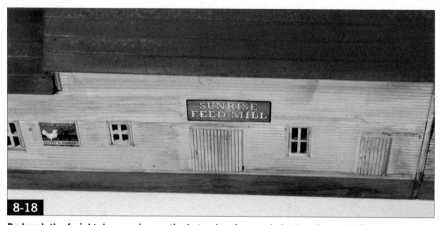

8-18

Drybrush the freight doors using vertical streaks of several shades of gray. This makes the paint on the doors look more worn than on the rest of the building.

8-17

Here's the wood loading platform after it has been drybrushed with light gray acrylic paint. The goal is to get just a hint of paint on the plastic. Be sure to move the brush along the grain, not across it.

were considered train-set quality. In recent years, several manufacturers have begun offering some fairly large and complex plastic structures in assembled form. These make it easy (albeit more expensive) to quickly fill a blank spot on the layout. And, with some careful attention to weathering, no one will ever know you didn't build the kit. I had a small Model Power brick building that simply needed some paint and weathering to make it look like it fits in with other more detailed structures (**8-14**). The Walthers Sunrise Feed Mill (**8-15**) is a more recent example of a factory-assembled structure.

The basic color scheme is believable, but it needs some additional weathering and personality to make it look like it didn't just come out of the box. I started by spraying the model with a coat of Testor's Dullcote. This kills the plastic sheen and provides some "tooth" to hold the rest of the weathering.

Next I brushed on a fairly heavy application of rubbing alcohol. This whitens the Dullcote, creating the look of sun-bleached roof panels. At first, this effect might look awful (**8-16**). Don't panic, this is only the first step!

Get some craft acrylic paints (Apple Barrel is one brand) that are a shade or two lighter than the wall and loading platform colors. I drybrushed these areas with the craft paint. To do this, dip the tips of the brush bristles in paint, then brush off most of the paint on a scrap piece of paper. Streak the brush across the model with the nearly dry brush. This technique can create a variety of realistic weathering effects (**8-17, 8-18**). Instead of attempting to

do the entire side of the model at once, use a small paintbrush to highlight individual boards.

The roof, since it's so visible, needs special attention. I used an assortment of watercolor pencils that were slightly more brown than the roof to highlight the edges of each panel along the seam. Then I brushed on some Bragdon Weathering Powders (**8-19**).

Individualizing structures

You can look upon a structure kit in one of two ways: as a collection of parts that can be assembled into a particular model or as a collection of walls, roofs, windows, doors, chimneys, and other raw parts. You can build the model straight from the box or use your imagination to combine the various components from one or more kits into a unique building.

Kitbashing helps get rid of the "I've seen that building before" syndrome that's so common with straight-from-the-box kits. Does that mean you shouldn't build any kits per their instructions? Of course not. You simply have to train yourself to look beyond the box label find ways to make your kit look less like everyone else's model.

Sometimes a new coat of paint is all it takes. Other times, more drastic measures are called for. Changing the use of a building to something other than what the kit maker intended is one way. For example, you can start with a kit for a hardware store, add a canopy to the front, make some new signs, and turn it into a restaurant. Or you could "borrow" the windows from a different kit to create a new look for

Photocopying tip

Many right-of-way structures are available in N scale. If you would rather build your own, plans for many have appeared in *Model Railroader* magazine and other publications over the years. If you should find plans published in a scale larger than N, simply place the original drawing on a photocopier and reduce the drawing to N scale. For example, if using an HO scale original, set the copier to 52.5 percent to reduce the plan to N scale. This will give you a plan that can serve as a template for building the model.

8-19

Watercolor pencils highlighted the roof panels and Bragdon Weathering powders worked well to tone down the roof. A wash of Micro-Mark Age-It-Easy Gray on all four walls helped blend all of the colors. The finished model looks right at home.

8-20

The only way the author could get a model of the Essex Junction, Vt., train shed/station was to scratchbuild it. The subwalls are styrene covered with Holgate & Reynolds HO scale brick. The bricks are a bit oversized for N scale, but look fine in person and in photos.

a building. Better still, use a different kit to add some walls made from a different material to disguise the kit's origins with a minimum of effort.

Scratchbuilding

Few words strike as much fear into the heart of many model railroaders as "scratchbuilding." However, there's no reason to be scared of scratchbuilding—just think of it as another useful addition to your bag of model railroading tricks. In many ways I find scratchbuilding to be easier than kitbashing.

The key to a successful scratchbuilding project is starting small and thinking in terms of what's included in a structure kit. Most kits include materials for walls, windows, doors, and roofs, and perhaps a photo of a finished model. When you scratchbuild a model you have to round up the materials you need and then find or create the "instructions." These can include a published plan or drawing, drawings you've made of a prototype building, or prototype photos.

An overwhelming selection of plastic and wood siding material is available. Also, a wide selection of door and window castings is offered by several manufacturers. When planning your scratchbuilding project don't let the label on the package fool you. A sheet of HO scale brick can often be used as concrete block in N scale. Likewise, a small or medium HO scale window

may be just what you need for a large N scale window for your project. Obviously, doors can't be adopted for different scales in the same manner.

In many cases scratchbuilding is the only way you can get that one perfect building for a layout that really sets the scene (**8-20**).

Specific scratchbuilding techniques are beyond the scope of this book, but you'll find helpful tips on scratchbuilding in almost every issue of *Model Railroader*. Just one piece of advice on scratchbuilding: Start small—don't attempt Grand Central Terminal as your first project. A small, simple building with four walls and a roof will get you familiar with the process. As your confidence grows, you'll be tackling bigger and more-complex projects. Before you know it, you'll be wondering why anyone is scared of scratchbuilding.

9-1

CHAPTER NINE

Meet the Androscoggin Central

It's a crisp, sunny autumn day on the N scale Androscoggin Central as a Central Vermont Alco RS-11 leads a Grand Trunk Railway train across the railroad's namesake river. Realistic, detailed scenes are possible on small as well as large N scale layouts.

Theme, prototype, and era, as well as size and space considerations, are all important factors in layout design. This chapter explains how I developed the theme for the Androscoggin Central layout shown here. You can skip ahead to the next chapter and start building if you wish, but unless you plan to duplicate this layout exactly (and how much fun would that be?) you'll be wise to consider these steps in designing your own layout. I considered a number of possible themes—more than a dozen as I recall—before deciding on the one shown in this book. One that almost made it to the construction stage was an ocean-side California layout on the Santa Fe's "Surf Line" between San Diego and Los Angeles— what a great setting for a prototype (and model) railroad!

I even went so far as to design a track plan and acquire some of the equipment that would be needed. But, it never made it to the construction stage. Maybe sometime in the future I'll build a layout with Santa Fe warbonnet diesels and fruit-packing houses, but it wasn't in the cards this time around.

In the end, I came back to a theme I had toyed with over the years but never actually built—the real Maine Central (MEC) Railroad of the 1970s and '80s. The resulting layout, which I named the Androscoggin Central, represents a fictional location along the MEC where it crosses the Androscoggin Central Railroad, a small short line that operates a former Central Vermont Alco RS-11 diesel. We are somewhere in northern New England—Maine or perhaps New Hampshire or Vermont. Guilford has just completed its take-over of the MEC, although not many locomotives and cars are wearing Guilford colors at this point.

I knew I wanted to include one large industry as a traffic source for the railroad. It's tempting to include a number of smaller industries on a model railroad, thinking this will add variety to the layout. But prototype railroads make their living serving large industries, so you will often find that a single large industry offers more potential for rolling stock variety and operating interest than a number of small industries. A paper mill seemed like an ideal choice for a single large industry.

On this (approximately) 4 x 8-foot layout, the Maine Central and Andro-scoggin Central cross each other at grade. Schematically, the railroad is two overlapping ovals with a hidden staging yard on one side of a low, tree-covered ridge that serves as a view block.

Before starting construction I spent a lot of time looking at photos of Maine Central scenes and equipment on various web sites and in books and magazines (9-2, 9-3).

I did not set out to model specific scenes. Instead I studied prototype photos and focused on selecting scenes, buildings, and other elements that looked as if they belonged in New England in the 1980s. My impression

A total of five Maine Central units, a trio of GP38s and a pair of GP7s, roll through Concord, Vt., on the Maine Central's famed Mountain Subdivision between St. Johnsbury, Vt., and Portland, Maine. The idea of a lot of trees with a town suddenly "appearing" inspired the arrangement of the town on the Androscoggin Central. *Jim Shaughnessy*

Nothing looks quite as a good as a train—model or prototype—crossing a bridge. The MEC crossed numerous bridges like this one, so including a scene representative of this type of a scene was an absolute given. *John M. Gould, author's collection*

of the MEC of the time was that of a relatively prosperous, well-run railroad. Like other New England railroads, the MEC preferred to keep older equipment in good repair, meaning this is not the place to find the latest six-axle power. In fact, the MEC didn't roster any six-axle road switchers until Guilford took over. This is a land of GP7s, RS-11s, GP38s, and, for variety, General Electrics: U18Bs and U25Bs.

As a railroad that derived the lion's share of its revenue from hauling paper and wood products, its most common car was the 50-foot boxcar.

Maine Central equipment is color-ful, meaning model railroad manufac-turers have not ignored the MEC. It's relatively easy to find a wide variety of accurate equipment painted and deco-rated in the railroad's paint schemes.

The rolling stock and locomotives are fairly straightforward, but struc-tures proved to be more problematic. Because this is a project layout, I didn't want to suggest scratchbuilding the structures, although it really wouldn't be that difficult and would improve the realism of the railroad. Instead I focused on kits that looked like they belonged, or at least didn't seem too out of place.

Deciding on the season was easy, at least for me. I wanted to set the layout

Evolution of the track plan

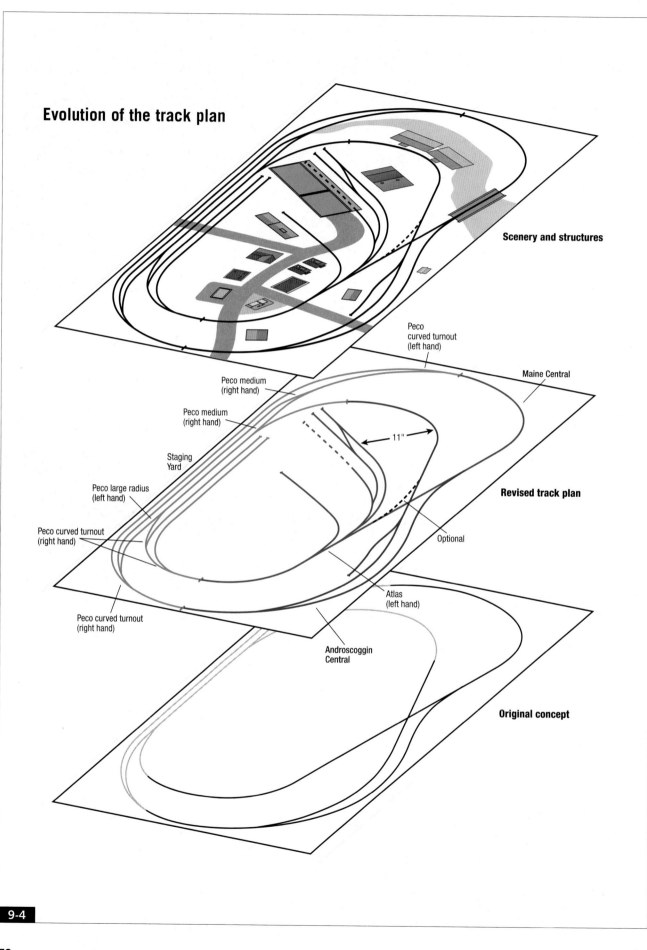

Scenery and structures

Peco
curved turnout
(left hand)

Maine Central

Peco medium
(right hand)

Peco medium
(right hand)

Staging
Yard

11"

Revised track plan

Peco large radius
(left hand)

Optional

Peco curved turnout
(right hand)

Atlas
(left hand)

Peco curved turnout
(right hand)

Androscoggin
Central

Original concept

9-4

9-5

This view shows the Androscoggin Central, looking west.

9-6

Here's a view of the west end of the layout, looking east.

in the brightly colored autumn, which New England is so famous for. Frankly, my trees are probably a little too colorful, but there's no denying the visual impact!

With my basic theme and setting decided upon, and the size of the layout determined (in my case a table roughly 4 x 8 feet) I started designing in earnest.

Developing the track plan

Since I knew I wouldn't be running long articulated steam locomotives or even six-axle diesels, I decided on a minimum radius of 12" for one end of each oval, with an 18" radius curve for the other end of each oval. The development of the track plan is in **9-4** (the final plan is on page 79). I started designing the railroad by drawing two overlapping ovals, each representing one railroad. I added several sidings and spurs to one side as the staging yard and an interchange between the two railroads on the foreground side.

I used a computer program (Adobe Illustrator) to draw the basic track positions, but there's no reason you couldn't use graph paper with some simple drafting tools (a pencil, straightedge, and compass are all you need).

With the basic track plan in place, I printed out several copies and used a pencil to sketch in some key signature elements I wanted to include, primarily an old brick mill building along a river, the track crossing the river, a small village, and, of course, the large central industry. The result of these sketches was enough to convince me that all of

9-7

Adding two Atlas no. 6 turnouts as shown will permit operating both railroads independently and will make it possible to interchange traffic from both directions. They are not essential, but the basic track geometry makes it easy to add them.

the components would fit and I could start building.

A key lesson is that when building a layout, don't let the initial plans hold you back when a better arrangement suggests itself. Comparing the sketches with the final track plan and the two aerial views of the layout (**9-5, 9-6**) will show I didn't build the layout exactly as drawn. In most cases I removed elements (see **2-8** in chapter 2) in an effort to allow as much breathing room as possible. Many times you'll discover that things that look good on paper aren't as appealing in reality.

Before we get started I should mention a couple of tracks I left out: a pair of turnouts that would allow both railroads to bypass the crossing. Adding these turnouts (**9-7**) will also permit operating both ovals as independent routes. I chose not to include them, but the track geometry would make these easy to include.

In the next two chapters we'll review how I built the Androscoggin Central. It's impossible to cover every possible construction detail, but you should be able to follow these steps to build a similar layout. You're welcome to do exactly as I did, but you'll be better off if you don't—after all, your railroad should reflect your own interests and personality.

Don't let the fact that I set the layout in 1980s New England limit you from modifying the plan to suit your interests. Substitute palm trees for pines and change the primary industry to a fruit packing house, and you could use this same track plan to model the Santa Fe in 1950s Southern California. Replace the large paper mill with brick structures and you could backdate the layout to the days of steam. Your only limit is your imagination. You could even expand the layout fairly easily if you ever get the bug—or the space.

10-1

Getting trains running

Capturing a slice of life is the goal of many model railroaders. We're heading into town on a crisp autumn morning when the quiet of a small New England town is broken by Maine Central U25B No. 234 leading a long freight train.

We all start building layouts by dreaming of wonderfully detailed scenes (10-1). But if a layout is to be truly rewarding to build and fun to operate, care must be taken during some of the more mundane stages of construction such as benchwork, track, and wiring. Rush these steps and you will regret it later. So, before we talk about scenicking and detailing the Androscoggin Central, let's build a solid, reliable railroad that works every time.

10-2

Ah, visions of grandeur yet to come! Here's the wood for the Androscoggin Central benchwork leaning against a wall in the layout room. If you don't have a way to accurately cut the larger sheet material, have the lumberyard do it for you.

10-3

A temporary construction station sits at one end of the basement family room where the layout would be located. A 4' x 4' piece of ¾" plywood across a pair of sawhorses serves as a table for the power miter saw.

10-4

The 2' x 4' base cabinet provides ample support for the railroad and provides some covered storage space under the layout.

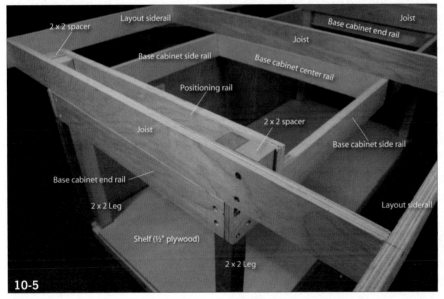

2 x 2 spacer
Layout siderail
Joist
Base cabinet end rail
Joist
Base cabinet side rail
Base cabinet center rail
Positioning rail
2 x 2 spacer
Joist
Base cabinet side rail
Base cabinet end rail
2 x 2 Leg
Layout siderail
Shelf (½" plywood)
2 x 2 Leg

10-5

Here's how all of the benchwork components fit with each other.

10-6

After cutting the legs to the desired height, drill holes in the bottom of the legs and hammer T-nuts into place.

10-7

Flathead carriage bolts screwed into the T-nuts make it easy to level the layout.

Benchwork

I've built a number of N scale railroads using hollow-core doors for benchwork, but since the Androscoggin Central was larger than any door I could find I decided to build my own benchwork. I intended to use 1 x 3 or 1 x 4 dimensional lumber (and you may certainly do so), but after spending an hour at the local home center trying to find more than a half-dozen straight pieces of wood, I gave up and bought a 4 x 8-foot sheet of ¾" birch plywood at a local lumberyard. I had the folks there rip the piece into 3"-wide strips, creating straight, knot-free 1 x 3s (**10-2**). You can do this yourself with a table saw or circular saw, but I was happy to pay the small charge to have it done, saving time and avoiding a great deal of sawdust.

At first I planned to keep the layout off the floor with a simple set of legs. However, remembering that I, like most model railroaders, always need more storage space (for construction and scenery materials while building the railroad and to hold all those extra cars and locomotives we inevitably collect once the railroad is operating), I decided to support the railroad on a base cabinet. Suffice to say you'll be shocked at the amount of "stuff" needed to build even a small layout. One of the unwritten laws of model railroading is the fact that a small layout needs just as many different items (ground foam colors, wire sizes and colors, tracklaying tools and supplies, etc.) as a large layout.

One key tool for accurately making square cuts in benchwork materials is a compound miter saw (**10-3**). Other very helpful tools include a cordless reversible variable speed drill, a small square, a level, and a jigsaw. The tools I used for benchwork construction are pretty straightforward and you may have most of them already.

In this chapter we'll get the Androscoggin Central up and running, working our way through benchwork, tracklaying, wiring, and even some basic scenery. Round up your tools and supplies and let's get started.

Step one: building a base cabinet

Storage space is always at a premium when building a model railroad, so I built a base cabinet (**10-4**) to support the layout.

Construction is fairly straightforward, and by following the pictures

10-8

A carpenter's square, clamped to a piece of plywood, helps keep the frame corners square.

10-9

Apply a bead of yellow carpenter's glue along the edge of the plywood frame member.

10-10

Drill pilot holes (countersunk in this case) and screw the two frame pieces together.

and text you should have no trouble building it. In **10-5** you can see how the layout gridwork fits onto the base cabinet. The layout is not screwed, bolted, or otherwise attached to the base cabinet—gravity alone holds the layout in place.

The size of the base isn't critical, but it's a good idea to make it a little narrower and shorter than the overall dimensions of the layout to allow some "foot space." Also, although this is an ideal benchwork approach for an island layout that might be moved once or twice (you could even build a new layout to fit atop this cabinet when you've completed this one!), I don't recommended it for layouts that go to shows on a regular basis: The cabinet, although moveable, is hardly what I'd call portable!

The height of the layout is determined by the length of the 2 x 2 legs (the final rail height will be the height of the legs + the thickness of the foam board + ¼" for the plywood). Carriage bolts in the bottom of the legs (**10-6, 10-7**) make it easy to level the layout.

The base cabinet consists of three 2 x 4-foot rectangular boxes secured at various heights along the legs. Be sure to leave enough of the top of the legs exposed to fit the layout double cross-spans in place (**10-5**). To keep the parts square, clamp a metal square in place on a flat level surface (**10-8**) and use the square when assembling the pieces.

All joints are glued and screwed. Run a bead of Elmer's Carpenter's Glue along the end of one of the pieces to be joined (**10-9**), place the two pieces inside the carpenter's square, drill pilot holes, and screw them together (**10-10**).

Once the base is assembled, add the shelves by notching the corners of two 2 x 4-foot sheets of ½" birch plywood. The bottom shelf should be fairly low to make the cabinet stable, and the middle shelf can be at any convenient height. Although I only added two shelves, you can add as many as you need (**10-11**). I covered three sides of the base with inexpensive beadboard paneling. This cleans up the appearance and adds stability to the base. You can also use plain ¼" plywood.

Layout grid

Construction of the layout benchwork itself is simple and straightforward. I assembled a grid of 1 x 3s with two sets of "double cross-spans" spaced to slip onto the top portion of the base cabinet legs (**10-11**). The cross-spans are made by sandwiching a small piece of 2 x 2 between two 1 x 3s. Adding some shim material (I used .080" styrene, but any similar shim could be used) will leave enough play in the cross spans so that they can easily be moved without being loose. Once I made sure that the grid fit atop the base cabinet, I screwed a piece of ¼" birch plywood to the grid and glued on a layer of ¾" foam board.

One of the keys to the Androscoggin Central's design is the typical New England mill waterfall in the river. The easiest way to do this is to add a second layer of ¾" foam board. The second foam layer also makes it easy to add gentle undulations to the terrain, breaking up the pool-table-level look of the rest of the layout. Rather than try and figure out the river location and cut the foam to fit, I simply glued a second sheet on top of the first, placed weights atop it overnight (books and model railroad magazines work well!), and waited until I'd located the track to cut the river into the top piece of foam.

At this stage (**10-12**) the layout looks more like a pink shelf than a model railroad.

Roadbed

I used Midwest N scale cork roadbed with Atlas flextrack (code 55 in visible areas and code 80 in the staging yards). With the exception of one Peco curved turnout on the visible portion of the railroad, all of the visible turnouts are Atlas code 55 and all the staging yard turnouts are Peco. (I used the Peco turnouts since they were the only curved turnouts available when I started. Atlas has since added a code 55 curved turnout to its line, and if I were starting this layout today I'd use Atlas code 55 throughout.)

Running cars with deep wheel flanges, including most older cars and virtually all Micro-Trains cars, will produce a noticeable clicking sound as the flanges hit the spike heads. Although

10-11

The finished layout frame will support the layout and provide storage space.

10-12

The base cabinet is covered with inexpensive beadboard paneling. The table—a piece of ¼" plywood and two layers of ¾" foam—makes a sturdy-yet-lightweight base for the railroad.

10-13

After positioning the 22.5-degree crossing, add the tracks that extend from each of the legs of the crossing. A straightedge keeps the flextrack aligned.

Installing Blue Point turnout throws

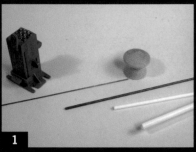

1

The components needed to install a Blue Point turnout control include the device itself, a length of 2-56 threaded rod, a Du-Bro Mini Kwik Link (part no. 228) to connect the rod to the Blue Point, a drawer pull, and some styrene tubing.

2

Start by marking the location of the throw rod on the foam board.

3

Drill a hole through both layers of foamboard and the plywood using a long (12") drill bit.

4

Ream the hole with a circular rasp to ensure that nothing will interfere with the throwing motion.

5

Mount the Blue Link mechanism under the table and add the throw rod and handle.

6

Once the Blue Point is installed, all you will see is a short length of wire sticking above the throw rods.

The Atlas turnouts don't have a built-in spring or latch mechanism to hold the points in place. It's a good idea to add some type of mechanism, either manual or electric, to ensure that the points stay in position.

In searching for a way to throw the turnouts that would be simple, reliable, and durable, I came across Blue Point turnout throws. (1).

Blue Points include a pair of built-in switches for powering frogs, a real plus with shorter wheelbase diesels and some steam engines. They are also small enough to fit completely within the benchwork frame without projecting beneath it.

The Blue Point turnout controls are easy to install and extremely reliable. I started by soldering wires to the Blue Point, figuring it was much easier to solder the wires now, when they were out in the open on my workbench. Mark the section under the throw rod on the foam board (2), then drill a hole through the foam and the ¼" plywood (3). A round rasp cleans the hole (4).

Mounting the turnout throw is best done with an assistant, but you can install one by yourself by using double-sided tape to hold the mechanism in place while you position it then permanently fasten it with no. 4 screws.

Bend the throw wire as shown and install the throw wire to the throw arm. It will be a little easier to install if the wire is cut longer than needed. Apply a strip of double-sided tape to the top of the Blue Point, place it under the layout, and slip the wire into the throw bar on the turnout from below. Before sticking the throw to the underside of the layout, move the lever with your thumb to confirm that it moves far enough to completely seat the points tightly against the stock rails in both directions. Then gently press the Blue Point in place against the layout. The double-sided tape will hold the device in place, but you still should secure it with at least two no. 4 screws (in opposite corners).

Add throw rods with 2-56 threaded rod (you can get this at a home-improvement store or from various online sources). Attach the rod using a Mini Kwik Link (made for radio-control cars and airplanes), sold by Du-Bro. Thread the rod into the Kwik Link and then snap it onto the Blue Point actuating arm.

Drill a hole through the fascia, then glue some styrene tube into the hole on the rear of the drawer pull with epoxy. Drill and tap the styrene 2-56 and screw it to the end of the 2-56 rod projecting from the fascia (5).

Blue Point offers flexible cable if you need to route the throw cable around curves. All the installations on this layout allowed straight paths between the Blue Point and fascia. Cut the throw wire to length with a wire cutter or cutoff disk (6). Use caution, since you don't want to damage the turnout.

the clicking noise is distracting and likely reduces the pulling power of locomotives due to the increased friction, I haven't had any operational problems running these wheels on the code 55 track. I do, however, plan to eventually replace all those wheelsets with low-profile or metal wheelsets.

The first step is to locate the track center lines for the cork roadbed. It's usually best to start with the most complex piece or area of track, in this case the 22.5-degree crossing where the two railroads cross. Set the crossing in the approximate position. Add the tangent track from the four legs of the crossing in place and pin the track temporarily (**10-13**).

Mark the radius of the curves (**10-14**). I used an Alkem laser-cut wood curve template for this, but you can just as easily make templates from pieces of cardboard. Once the center line of the curve is marked, connect it to the center line of the tracks coming from the crossing. Some cosmetic curves, which were obviously broader than the 18" radius, are necessary to get everything to look right and fit.

With the track center lines marked, the cork roadbed can be added. This material is readily available, easy to use, and produces a smooth surface. It also reduces the noise the trains make (although N scale trains are pretty quiet to begin with). Start by splitting the cork roadbed in half. Spread some glue (I used Dap Adhesive clear caulk, but carpenter's glue also works) on either side of the track center line. There's a straight and sloped side to each cork piece. Place the straight side of the cork along the center line and hold it in place with push pins (**10-15**) while the glue sets.

Place the second half of the cork snugly against the section that's already in place (**10-16**). Be sure to overlap the ends of the two halves slightly (at least 1"-2").

At turnouts, start by laying a cork strip through one route of the turnout, just as you did for normal track (**10-17**). Once the glue has dried, place the cork for the diverging route in position with a little overlap and cut through both layers of cork with a sharp hobby

10-14

Curve templates from Alkem Scale Models helped in marking the mainline curves. Connect them with the tangent lines from the crossing.

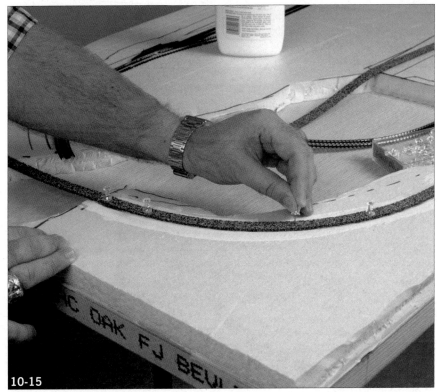

10-15

Spread a thin coat of adhesive and place the first section of cork along the track center line. Secure it with push pins.

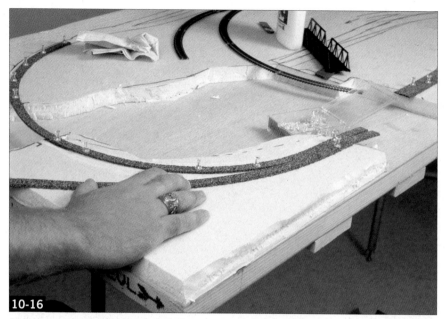

10-16

Add the other half of the cork roadbed and secure it with push pins.

10-17

For turnouts, start by tracing the outline of the turnout directly on the foam board. Install the cork for the straight route as you would for single track.

10-18

After the glue has dried on the straight route, place the cork in position for the diverging route. Hold it in place while trimming it to fit with a sharp hobby knife and glue in place.

10-19

Setting the actual structures in place (this is the Walthers paper mill) helps locate the related trackwork.

Joining Peco turnouts to Atlas track

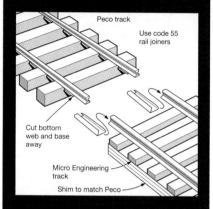

There are several places where I needed to join Peco turnouts to Atlas code 55 track. Peco streamlined code 55 track isn't truly code 55 rail: Although the visible portion above the tie is .055" tall with a realistic profile, it has a hidden base buried in the ties. This means it can't be joined to other rail with conventional rail joiners.

To solve this problem, trim away the bottom section of rail (below the code 55 base) with a cutoff disk in a motor tool (be sure to wear eye protection) Then cut away the lower web and file the rail to a true code 55 height. Then use three shims of .010" styrene to even the ties and join the Peco and Atlas track using an Atlas rail joiner.

The ties are different dimensions, but once the rail is painted and ballasted the difference is hard to spot.

knife. Repeat the process with the other half of the cork roadbed (**10-18**).

The next step is to locate the sidings and spurs for the various industries, especially the paper mill. I assembled the Walthers paper mill to a point that I could place it on the layout and accurately locate the appropriate tracks, especially the siding that runs into the building (**10-19**).

Once the glue dries completely, use a sanding block (**10-20**) to gently smooth the surface of the cork and to remove the "shoulder" that remains

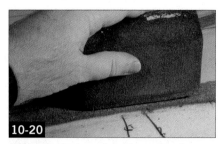

10-20

A sanding block smooths the cork and removes any remaining jagged edges on the angled shoulder that remain from splitting the cork in half.

10-21

Terminal rail joiners have been placed on one route of a turnout. Drill matching holes through the cork and layout table.

from splitting the cork in half. Jagged bits of cork at this angled shoulder can play havoc with ballasting later.

Track

The Alas code 55 track looks good, is easy to work with, and results in smooth, flowing trackwork. Its appearance is much closer to scale than the older Atlas line of code 80 track. Atlas also offers a wide assortment of sectional track in its code 55 line, which may be an option if you don't want to deal with flextrack.

Start laying track by pinning the turnouts in place. Since the Atlas turnouts don't have a positive locking throwbar, you'll want to add some type of turnout throw mechanism to hold the points in place. I chose Blue Point manual throws (the sidebar on page 76 explains how I installed these). Once the turnouts are in position, the rest of the tracklaying consists of connecting the turnouts with lengths of flextrack.

Bend the flextrack to fit, centering it over the cork roadbed. Unless the track is dead straight, one rail will slip through the ties and end up longer than the other. Take your time and

make sure that curves are smooth, with no sudden jogs or bends.

Use a hobby knife to notch the longer rail at the point that's even with the shorter rail and trim away any ties that

will interfere with the cut. I prefer rail nippers for cutting flextrack. Align the face of the nippers with the notch and cut the rail to length. The nippers produce a smooth cut, but you'll still need

Androscoggin Central track plan

Peco Curved turnout (left hand)

Alkem mill (2)

Maine Central

Peco medium (right hand)

Walthers paper mill

Peco medium (right hand)

11"

Micro Engineering bridge (2)

Walthers Sunrise Feed Mill

Staging Yard

Optional

Branchline farm outbuilding

Atlas houses

Branchline Dubois Store

Walthers State Line Supply

Peco large radius (left hand)

Walthers shed

Alkem Jake's Gas

Atlas (left hand)

City Classics gas station

Peco Curved turnout (right hand)

Androscoggin Central

Peco Curved turnout (right hand)

AMB Ellington Mercantile

Grid lines are 6" apart

Painting track

Shiny rails don't contribute to realism, and really wreak havoc with photography!

The painted rail looks far better than shiny, unpainted rail. You can follow this first coat with a wash of diluted paint to blend the ballast and track together.

The angled tips on the Floquil paint markers make it easy to paint the sides of the rails. I applied Rail Tie Brown, followed by Rust, to both sides of the rails. Don't worry if some of the paint gets onto the ties and tie plates since they duplicate the appearance of those parts of prototype track.

One of the best ways to improve the look of any model railroad is to paint the track. Look at real railroad track and you'll notice the ties and rails are usually any color but the shiny silver with plastic brown or black ties of model track. I usually paint the track and rail after adding the basic scenery texture but before ballasting the track.

In the past I've used an airbrush, and although the method works well, it can be a messy project—the thought of spilling paint or getting overspray on our newly carpeted basement family room sent me looking for a better option. That's when I discovered Floquil paint markers at the local hobby shop. Floquil even makes a set of three markers in a "track weathering pack." These made it easy to paint and weather the track without a lot of mess.

10-22

Adhesive works well for securing track to cork. Dap adhesive caulk goes on white but dries clear.

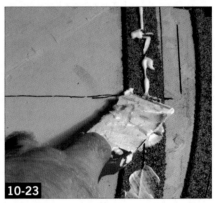

10-23

Before installing the track, smooth the caulk into a thin coat on the cork with a putty knife.

10-24

Here's the track in place at the paper mill. The caulk sets slowly, allowing time to align the track.

to clean the edges. File the bottom, top, and web of the rail smooth.

Slip rail joiners on the rail ends. Most joints require standard joiners, but for points where wires are required add terminal joiners (**10-21**) and for insulated joints use plastic insulated joiners. (See the track diagram on page 82 for the locations of the terminal and insulated joiners.)

I glued my track in place with Dap adhesive caulk (**10-22**). Many modelers opt for small nails to secure track, but the nail heads remain visible—especially in close-up photos. I prefer glue, which works well and provides an invisible method of securing track.

Apply a bead of caulk down the center of the roadbed and smooth it with a putty knife into a relatively thin coat (**10-23**).

Place the track in position. Although the caulk grabs the track pretty quickly, you still have a surprising amount of working time to get the final position correct. Make sure there are no kinks or bends and that curves are smooth. Once everything is aligned, hold the track in place with push pins (**10-24**). The caulk turns clear as it dries.

Take your time when laying track. Test-fit each piece of track before gluing it in place. Make sure all rail joints are square and that all rail ends rest securely in their joiners. Trim or file rail ends as needed.

Adding a riverbed

Since rivers, bridges, and old mills are all signature elements of New England railroads, it made sense to include all three and create a signature scene for

the railroad. Foam construction makes it easy to add the river at any time. I cut the river channel during tracklaying, although I could have easily done it after all the track was laid. In fact, as we'll see in the next chapter, I modified the shape of the river slightly once the basic scenery was in place. Foam construction makes such changes easy.

I originally considered having the main line cross the river twice by running it off the right side of the layout. Instead, I decided it would allow some additional scenery options to have the river run behind the mill building and hill, gradually disappearing from sight.

Model railroaders love bridges, but a common problem is that many model railroad bridges span distances so short that the prototype would never build a bridge in a similar situation. To avoid the too-short-bridge look, even on this fairly small layout, I used two bridges to cross a wide span—close to an actual foot. I made the bridges from two Micro-Engineering 50-foot girder bridge kits (**10-25**).

Since I wanted to include a waterfall by an old mill, I cut away one layer of the ¾" foam above the dam and removed both layers (all the way down to the plywood) for the remainder of the river. Rough locations are fine for now, and if you're not sure how wide you want the river to be, leave some extra material in place—it's easy to cut away additional foam later. A utility knife made quick work of cutting out the foam (**10-26**).

I originally planned to use Chooch bridge abutments and piers—and you can certainly do so—but the resin parts will need to be cut down to size. Instead, I built two concrete abutments from .060" styrene (**10-27, 10-28**). They're based on prototype abutments I've seen in photos of the Maine Central. With the riverbed cut to shape I installed the bridge pier and abutments. We'll discuss finishing this scene in detail in the next chapter.

10-25

Micro-Engineering bridges marked the width of the riverbed where the railroad crosses the river. The outline of the river and the mill building are visible. The author decided not to use the Chooch cut-stone abutments shown here.

10-26

A utility knife made quick work of removing the foam from the riverbed. The top layer of foam is trimmed farther back than the lower one to create a gently sloping riverbed.

10-27

10-28

The simulated concrete abutments (left) were built from .060" styrene. After cutting the cast-resin Chooch cut stone pier to the proper height (right), it was painted with a mixture of dark gray and black craft paint.

Wiring diagram

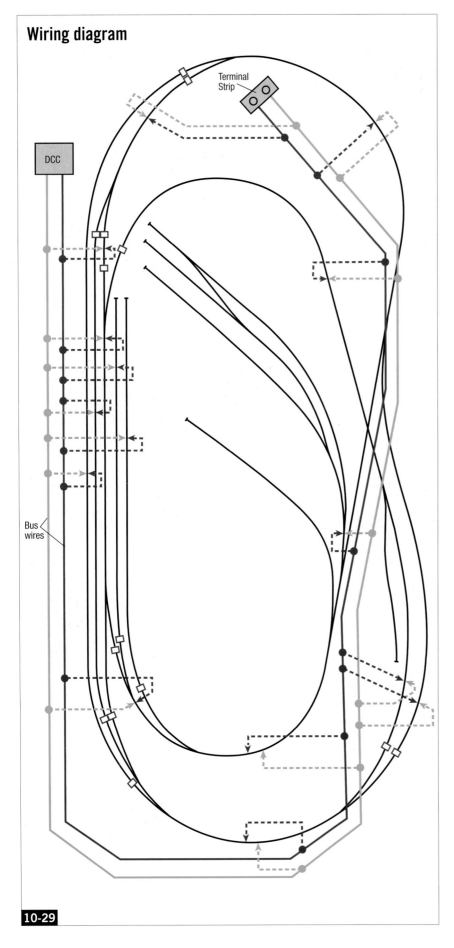

Terminal Strip

DCC

Bus wires

Wiring

I wired the layout as shown in **10-29**. I decided to color-code the wires. Sure, it's easy to keep track of where each of those wires are heading as you install them—especially on a small layout—but it's a different matter to be able to come back months or even years later and troubleshoot the wires. The easiest way to make those future headaches less painful is to identify the wires. The colors of the wires are not important—electricity doesn't care if the wire is blue, white, or red! Consistency is, however, critical. Here's my color-code system:

Red: Bus wire 1 (on the inside, or "R"ear rail when looking at the layout.

Black: Bus wire 2 (outside rail when looking at layout)

Green: Between turnout frogs and turnout throws (green, since frogs are, well, green).

Use a permanent marker to scribble this code underneath the layout where you'll easily see it when you look underneath to check the wiring.

Start at the shelf where the controls (in this case a Digital Command Control system) will be located. Run a pair of bus wires around the perimeter of the layout and dead-end them at a terminal strip. If you ever expand the layout, you can connect the next bus wire segment to that terminal strip.

I joined the feeder wire from each terminal rail joiner from the track to terminal strips (I bought long terminal strips and cut them into blocks of two, since only two wires were needed for each block). From the terminal strip I ran a length of heavier wire to the bus wire. You can solder the feeder wires to the terminal strips. It's a lot of work, as you have to strip the insulation from the bus wire in many locations, but produces very reliable connections.

Instead I opted for Insulation Displacement Connectors (IDCs), also called "suitcase" connectors, **10-30**. The photo with the Blue Point turnout controllers on page 76 shows these in place. They are easy and fast to use. Slip one over the bus wire, put the feeder wire in the other hole, and squeeze the connector in place with pliers (**10-31**).

At this point you can connect a conventional DC throttle and enjoy

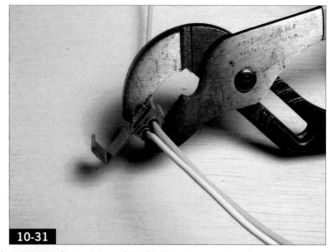

Insulation-displacement connectors (IDCs, or "suitcase connectors") join a feeder wire to a bus wire with the squeeze of a pliers.

10-32

The Digitrax Super Chief system rests under the layout. The command station (center), power supply (left), and a handheld throttle.

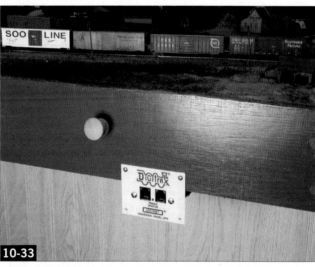

10-33

The author installed a throttle jack (the Digitrax UP5 Universal Panel) to the front of the layout.

operating trains on the layout. Even if you plan to add a DCC system from the start as I did, it's a good idea to test the layout with an ordinary DC power pack. Ideally, you should test-run a train as you wire each section of track. That way, if things stop working, you know where to start looking for the problem. Connect the bus wires to the variable DC terminals on the power pack, place a non-decoder-equipped (or dual-mode) locomotive on the track, and turn on the throttle. The engine should move.

If things don't work properly, now is the time to find out why. Check the obvious first: Did you connect the correct wires together? Were you consistent with the color scheme? (Don't ask how I know to check this!) Make sure you don't leave any metal tools sitting across the rails.

If the connections are good, the problem may be with the turnouts. If you used Electro-Frog turnouts and you notice the trains aren't working in one section of track, or you are getting a short-circuit indication on the power pack, the most likely problem is a missing insulated gap. As mentioned earlier, you need to add insulated rail joiners at the places shown on the track diagram with Peco Electro-Frog turnouts (yet another reason to use Atlas turnouts throughout!).

With all the connections made and tested, you should be able to run a locomotive around the entire layout. Electrically, the railroad is one big block at this point.

It's now time to add the DCC system. I chose a Digitrax Super Chief (**10-32**). The Super Chief is a high-end

system for such a small layout, but I already had one on hand from an earlier layout, and I also wanted to make sure the control system would have the capability to handle an expanded version of the layout. I also added a utility throttle for a second engineer.

On the staging yard side of the railroad, operators can plug into the command station. To make it easier to control trains from either side of the railroad, I installed a Digitrax throttle jack panel (**10-33**) on the front of the layout.

Spend some time just running trains and having fun with the layout. Make sure trains run smoothly through turnouts and all of the other trackwork. When everything is in order, move to the next chapter and we'll get to work on some scenery.

11-1

CHAPTER ELEVEN

Adding scenery and details to the Androscoggin Central

On a crisp October afternoon a trio of Harvest Gold Maine Central diesels, two GP38s and a U25B, leads train JR-2 across the Androscoggin River. Scenery is critical to capturing a slice of life like this one. While it may seem intimidating at first, creating an appealing scene that will wow your family and friends is fun and easy.

Even in the ready-to-run model railroading world of today, you can't buy completed scenery at the hobby shop—you still have to make it. Scenery is all about artistic expression. The benchwork, track, and wiring are the skeleton of a model railroad, but the scenery gives it the visual impact that will set it apart from every other model railroad and make it uniquely your own. Replace my tree-covered hillsides (11-1) with rock outcroppings and scrub pines and add different structures, and your version of the Androscoggin Central could easily be the New Mexico Northern.

Many beginning—and a surprising number of veteran—model railroaders think building scenery is beyond their abilities. They believe they need to be artists to create satisfying scenery. That simply isn't true. Scenery is easy and a lot of fun. The step-by-step instructions in this chapter will get you started, but for more details on building scenery be sure to refer to Dave Frary's outstanding book, *How to Build Model Railroad Scenery*.

Basic landforms and texturing

When building the benchwork I removed some foam board from the riverbed. I used those pieces and an extra piece of foam to build up the hills and ridges on the layout. I cut the foam pieces to the approximate shape of the ridge and stacked them like a wedding cake before securing them (**11-2**) to each other and to the layout with Power Grab foam board adhesive (available at Home Depot and other home improvement centers).

Arrange the hills in an appealing, realistic manner. Be careful not to put the hillsides too close to the tracks, especially around curves, and pay attention to the clearance between the terrain and the track. The main ridge on the Androscoggin Central stands no more than 4" at its tallest point. You can make the slope of the forested hillsides relatively steep, since the trees will lessen the apparent steepness of the slope.

After the glue dries, carve the hillsides to shape. I've used hot-wire cutters and hot craft knives to cut foam on previous projects, but these produce noxious fumes. For this layout I used a drywall saw (which is basically a large

11-2

A low ridge separates the staging yard from the foreground section of the railroad. The bound volumes of *Model Railroader* make ideal weights to hold the foam pieces in place while the glue sets overnight.

11-3

The author used a variety of knives and saws, including this Stanley Surform tool, to carve the foam into realistic land contours. Fill any gaps with lightweight joint compound.

11-4

Paint and texture materials cover any imperfections in the foam surface.

11-5

Apply a relatively thick coat of inexpensive earth-color latex paint to the layout. Sprinkle on a variety of shades and textures of ground foam. This is simply a first layer to hide all that pink!

11-6

Sprinkle some Highball light and dark earth over the dirt roads and parking lots.

11-7

Soak the ground with rubbing alcohol. An eyedropper or small pipette, like this one, makes it easy to control where the alcohol goes.

11-8

With the alcohol still wet, apply a 1:1 mix of Elmer's white glue and water over the scenery materials.

11-9

If the ground texture appears too rough or coarse when it dries, smooth it with a sanding block.

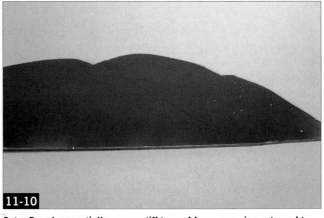

11-10

Gator Board, essentially a very stiff type of foam core, is contoured to form distant mountain ridges. Start by marking the hillsides and cutting the board with a utility knife.

serrated knife), finer hobby saws, utility knives, and various Stanley Surform tools as in **11-3**.

The disadvantage of these tools is that they produce a lot of foam dust, which seems to cling to everything. Have a shop vacuum around to clean up the mess.

Fill any small gaps between the pieces of foam with lightweight joint compound (ordinary joint compound will crack when it dries). It isn't necessary to cover the foam with plaster—paint and texturing material will hide the surface (**11-4**). Apply a thick coat of earth-colored latex paint to the hillsides with a cheap paintbrush (**11-5**). It's not a bad idea to cover the track with masking tape to protect it from paint splatters.

While the paint is still wet, sprinkle on various shades and textures of ground foam. The idea is to get a basic scenery layer down to cover the pink foam. We'll be adding different texture and coloring materials later as part of the finishing scenery.

For the dirt parking lots, start by sprinkling on a combination of Highball dark and light earth. You can also use finely sifted real dirt (**11-6**). Soak the dirt with ordinary rubbing alcohol applied with a pipette (**11-7**). When the texture material is completely saturated, dribble on a 1:1 mixture of Elmer's white glue and water (**11-8**). If

the dirt beads up, the glue mix is too thick—add more water. The Highball dirt is so fine that it will sometimes dry too rough and bumpy to represent even a rough N scale parking lot. If that's the case, sand the dirt surface with a sanding sponge designed for sanding drywall seams (**11-9**).

Hill boards

To give even greater depth the scenery, add profile boards cut to the shape of distant mountain tops between the visible layout and the staging yards. These take up little space (just the thickness of the material), but add tremendous visual depth. They also hide the staging yards from view.

11-11

Spray the hill boards with inexpensive dark green paint. Once dry, coat the boards with spray adhesive.

11-12

Sprinkle ground foam on the still-tacky adhesive. The "closer" hill is duplicated with coarse ground foam in the same color as the foreground trees. Distant hills are covered with fine green foam to represent more far-off hillsides.

11-13

I thought the river looked too narrow, so I widened the channel by trimming away more foam and then carving the new bank to shape with a Stanley Surform tool.

11-14

A piece of foam core cut to match the footprint of the mill provides a flat, level surface for the structure.

11-15

Paint the foundation a light concrete color. Cut random stress fractures into the "concrete" with a hobby knife.

11-16

A wash of black shoe dye and rubbing alcohol fills the cracks and darkens the surface.

Fall trees

1 Remove the raw SuperTree from the package and spray-paint the armature.

2 Soak the armatures in diluted matte medium.

3 Sprinkle ground foam onto the armature.

4 Hang the finished tree on a clothesline to dry. If the trunk is bent, clip a weight (such as tweezers) to the tree while the matte medium dries.

5 Bend the armatures to shape. The plastic base won't be installed on the layout but it's handy for keeping the tree upright while you're gluing the foliage in place.

6 Here's a completed foreground tree, ready for installation on the layout.

Most of the questions I've gotten from fellow modelers who have seen pictures of the Androscoggin Central have centered on the trees. I set the Androscoggin Central in the late fall, when the trees are a riot of color, but did so with a great deal of trepidation. Be forewarned, fall scenery can easily be overdone—it's easy to produce a cartoonish imitation of reality. It would actually be a very rare autumn to see trees looking as full and colorful as they do on this model railroad. But one of the best parts about model railroading is the way we can have those wonderful fall colors (which in truth may only appear once a decade in the real world!) along with a bright blue "Kodachrome" sky.

I have been experimenting with fall scenery for more than a decade and am only now starting to be pleased with the results. The best advice I can offer is (1) keep everything to the same basic tone—lots of brown, rust, and deep red, OR yellows and oranges (this is very easy to overdo); (2) be sure to include green—about half of my trees are some shade of green; and (3) be sure to include green. Yes, I know I said it twice—it's that important.

There are two types of trees on the layout: "background" trees, which are those found along the ridge and clustered around the buildings and along the tracks; and foreground or specimen trees, which stand alone or in prominent locations. All told, there are close to 500 individual trees on this small layout, and there are a few spots were I could add more.

Keep real trees in mind as you make and plant model trees. Mature trees can easily grow 80 to 100 feet in height, and many model railroaders are reluctant to use such tall trees. I suggest adding a few trees that indeed tower realistically over buildings and trains, but remember forced perspective works well on layouts. For example, the trees on the Androscoggin Central range in height from 35 scale feet in the background to 60 to 80 scale feet tall in the foreground. Placing some shorter trees in the foreground is fine, but a tall tree would really look out of place next to the shorter trees in the background.

Another good rule to keep in mind when planting trees is to arrange groupings in odd numbers. I don't know why, but two trees together don't look "right," while three or five look just fine. Also remember you need to have access to the trains (to reach in and uncouple cars, for example), so be sure to leave the trees a little farther from tracks that will be worked regularly. Likewise, keep in mind clearance requirements when planting trees along the tracks.

Background trees

I used these all over the railroad, including at the front. As you're making trees it will become obvious which armatures will make great stand-alone trees and which are better suited as "fillers" for the ridge line.

I start with Scenic Express SuperTrees with Scenic Express fine ground foam. I like to use a variety of fall foliage colors, although I prefer the "clay" and "earth" tones for the trees.

Start by painting the armatures with inexpensive Krylon camouflage spray paint (1). When that dries, soak them in diluted matte medium (2) and sprinkle them with ground foam from above (3). Don't just dip the trees in the foam, as that will cover up much of the fine branch structure that makes the SuperTrees look good. Hang the trees upside down to dry (a clothesline works well, 4), then plant them on the layout.

Foreground trees

The one glaring flaw with SuperTrees are their spindly trunks. To create trees with heavier trunks and branches, apply SuperTree foliage to Woodland Scenics plastic tree armatures.

After bending the Woodland Scenics armatures to shape, paint them with Krylon Camouflage followed by a wash of light gray. While the paint is drying, go through your SuperTree "leftovers"— odd pieces that were too small to use even as background trees—and divide them by color.

Making foreground trees takes some time, but it's not difficult. Place a few drops of cyanoacrylate adhesive (CA) on a piece of scrap plastic. Then, with tweezers, dip the end of a piece of foliage in the CA and apply it to the armature (5). The first few pieces may be tricky to keep in place, but as you build up the foliage the tree will hold together very well. The completed foreground trees (6) look great when placed next to a building or along the road.

11-17
To make the river banks, apply some rocks and sand for texture (like the Scenic Express river rock shown here). Position the rocks with a soft brush until everything looks right.

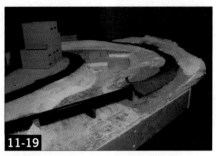
11-19
Apply a skim coat of lightweight joint compound to the river bed to seal any gaps and to hide the grain on the plywood base.

Make the hill boards by marking the approximate shape of distant mountains on several scrap pieces of flat material. I used ⅛" Gator Board (11-10) since I had it on hand, but Masonite hardboard or foam core would also work. Once the hillsides are cut to shape, paint them green, coat them with spray adhesive (11-11), and sprinkle on coarse ground foam (11-12) to represent nearby hills and fine ground foam to represent more distant hillsides.

Slip the boards in place behind the ridge separating the staging yard from the visible portion of the layout. Barbecue skewers stuck in the foam board surface of the layout prop up the hill boards as needed.

Building a river and waterfall

The river, with an old brick mill building clinging to the bank, is certainly the scenic focal point of the layout. The two layers of foam that make up the basic tabletop made it easy to add the river and the signature mill falls. We already covered how I made the riverbed and bridge crossing when we discussed the benchwork.

11-18
Wet the rocks with rubbing alcohol, then secure the ground texture material with a mix of white glue and water.

11-20
The riverbed is painted black to represent deeper water. Feather in some tan paint along the banks to represent shallower areas.

This is one of those cases where the structure is such an integral part of the scene that it needs to be completed before you can blend it into the scenery. I made the basic building from two Alkem Scale Models kits combined into one long building and angled to match the course of the river. I placed the completed model in the scene (11-13) and could tell immediately that the river looked too narrow. I was able to easily and quickly widen the river about 2" with a utility knife, making the scene look far more natural.

To support the mill, I made a flat foam core foundation that juts into the river. I placed the model on a sheet of foam core, traced the outline of the structure, and cut it out with sharp hobby knife. This provided a flat base for the mill and allowed me to accurately locate the building and its foundation without constantly handling the model.

After gluing the foam core foundation in place with carpenter's glue, I filled any gaps between the foam core and river with scraps of foam board. Once the glue dried, I smoothed and blended everything with lightweight

11-21

The author glued rock castings at the waterfall itself and to represent rocks protruding above the water surface just downstream.

11-22

Turbulent water is easy to add by drybrushing highlights downstream from the rocks, at the base of the falls, and at a few random points to simulate underwater obstructions.

11-23

Begin making the waterfall by running a bead of clear caulk along the top of the rocks.

11-24

A scrap piece of stripwood makes an ideal tool to pull the caulk "water" straight down to the river surface below.

joint compound (Sculptamold or plaster would also work), **11-14**.

I painted the foundation to look like concrete (**11-15**). I scribed stress fractures into the concrete with a hobby knife, then added a wash of alcohol and India ink (about one teaspoon of ink in a bottle of rubbing alcohol) to bring out the details and tone down the concrete color (**11-16**).

All the rework and "earth moving" meant repainting the riverbed using inexpensive black acrylic craft paint. I applied some relatively coarse (for N scale) river rock—in this case, Scenic Express River Gravel (No. S3100-3) to the river banks (**11-17**).

After soaking the texture material with rubbing alcohol, I applied a generous coat of "lightly" diluted white glue

(about 60 percent glue and 40 percent water, with a few drops of dishwashing detergent as a flow agent) to the rocks along the riverbank (**11-18**).

I waited to add the final "water" to the river and waterfall until the various scenic textures had been added along the riverbank, as gluing ground foam in place after a water surface has been poured can result in a big mess.

Start by applying a skim coat of lightweight joint compound to prevent any grain from the plywood showing through the finished river surface (**11-19**). Once the joint compound dries, lightly sand it smooth.

The next step is to paint the river surface with ordinary black acrylic paint (**11-20**). After the black paint dries, brush some light tan paint on

the river banks to represent shallow water. Feather the brown paint where it meets the black—the colors should be blended, with no harsh edge showing between them.

Water rushing over rock waterfalls is a signature item of New England mill streams, making this an effect well worth duplicating. I placed the falls at the point where the plywood riverbed meets the single layer of foam board. I cast several plaster rocks from Woodland Scenics small rock molds, adding these at the "drop" itself. For variety, I also added several rocks to the riverbed downstream from the falls to duplicate larger rocks that are exposed above the water. Once I was satisfied with the arrangement (**11-21**), I glued the rock castings in place with white glue.

11-25

Pour a small amount of Realistic Water on the riverbed. Wait to see how much area it covers before adding more liquid.

11-26

An inexpensive foam brush works well for spreading the Realistic Water around rocks and up to the banks.

11-27

Thick acrylic gloss medium makes it easy to build up waves. The material dries clear with a glossy surface to match the Realistic Water. Avoid getting bubbles in the medium as you shape the waves.

11-28

Apply a coat of full-strength white glue to ground areas that will eventually be covered with trees.

Once the glue had dried, I painted the rocks with dark gray acrylic craft paint. After the paint dried I lightly drybrushed them with earth-colored latex paint. When doing this, hit the rocks lightly with the brush, with just enough paint to barely highlight the surface texture.

You can capture the look of turbulent water around the rocks and at the base of the falls by drybrushing an acrylic paint mixture of 1 part black, 1 part Payne's Gray, and 8 parts white to the areas where turbulent water would be found on the downstream sides of the various rocks and other river obstructions (**11-22**). Keep the drybrushed effects parallel to one another, since that will enhance the illusion of water current.

To make the waterfall, apply a fairly thick bead of clear acrylic caulk (the same caulk used to hold the track in place) along the top of the waterfall, just above the rocks (**11-23**). Pull the caulk over the falls toward the river surface below with a small piece of scrap stripwood. This is easier than it sounds—the only trick is to keep the caulk plumb so the "water" is falling straight down, and not at an angle.

Many commercial water materials are available, but I chose Woodland Scenics Realistic Water for the basic layer, with acrylic gloss medium over it to create waves. Over several months and one move (which included a month in an non-air-conditioned garage at the height of a muggy, hot, Virginia summer), I haven't had any

problems with the water becoming discolored or cracking.

Carefully pour a thin coat of Realistic Water into the river bed (**11-25**). Don't pour it along the riverbanks, since it can creep up on the banks and leave a glossy area in the worst possible location. I found it easiest to pour a thin coat of the material in the middle of the river, allowing it to spread out to the banks. The water won't flow into all the small crevices, so you'll need to persuade it with a small sponge brush (**11-26**). Gently brush the material in place with slow, smooth strokes. Don't brush it too vigorously, or the result will be unrealistic bubbles in the surface when it dries.

Once the Realistic Water dries completely, add some wave texture with

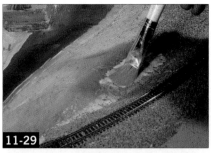

11-29

An inexpensive paintbrush works well for spreading glue around the areas that will be covered by fallen leaves.

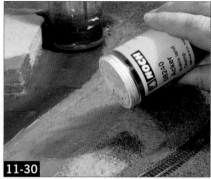

11-30

Apply the leaf material over the white glue.

11-31

The forest floor is now ready for the trees.

11-32

11-33

Scenic Express farm pasture blend and Woodland Scenics harvest gold were used for most of the grass texture. Special static-grass applicators are available, but the Noch bottles work well.

base with earth-colored latex paint, I consider that a first coat. Much can be done to enhance the appearance of the ground cover.

Forest floors are covered with a deep blanket of fallen leaves. To add the woodland ground cover, locate all of the areas that will eventually be covered with trees (you don't have to be precise). Apply a thin coat of full-strength white glue (**11-28**) with an inexpensive paintbrush (**11-29**), then add the leaves themselves. You can use any number of commercial products for this, or you can easily (and inexpensively make your own by grinding actual dried leaves in a blender or using tea leaves. I used a flocking product from Noch called "Arable Land" (**11-30**). Once the leaf texture dries (**11-31**), the layout is ready for the trees (see page 88).

Electrostatic grass and Silflor

For the open areas I used a variety of electrostatic grasses from Woodland Scenics and Silflor. I also used Silflor grass mats and prairie tufts. The complete line of Silfor products is available from Scenic Express. At first I planned to use these products to complement the more typical ground foam. Since they were easy to work with and looked so good I ended up using a lot more of them on the open (non-forested) areas.

I used two colors of static grass, Scenic Express Farm Pasture Blend and Woodland Scenics Harvest Gold (**11-32**), for the majority of the open areas of the layout. You can buy special static-grass applicators, but it's not really necessary for the small areas on this railroad. The Noch applicator bottles have lids with holes in them which help the individual fibers of grass stand up when they're applied to the base. Although they don't work as well as the special applicators, the bottles are much less expensive and work well.

To apply the static grass, spread white glue onto the painted scenery base (or on top of the existing ground foam). Load the static grass into the applicator bottle (**11-33**). Then, in one motion, move the applicator toward the layout and squeeze the bottle, shooting the fibers onto the glue. Keep the

acrylic Gloss Medium (**11-27**). This thick, gel-like material holds its shape and dries clear, making it perfect for adding wave texture and "movement" atop the Realistic Water, which dries level. Keep the wave heights reasonable—a mill stream shouldn't look like a North Atlantic hurricane is blowing

through town. I also took care to run the wave pattern perpendicular to the riverbank, since it enhances the illusion of the water current.

Adding additional ground textures

Although I added a basic layer of ground foam when I painted the foam

11-34

Blending two or more colors of electrostatic grass will produce realistic results. Here some faded greens with the addition of yellows duplicates an eastern appearance of late summer or early fall grass.

11-35

Silflor grass is a perfect addition along a building foundation, like this small farm shed built from a Branchline Trains laser kit.

11-36

Spread a thin layer of full-strength white glue to areas where you want to apply the grass.

11-37

Here's the grass mat before stretching and separating.

11-38

After gently teasing the Silflor mat, press the material into the glue. Blend the mat as desired into the surrounding terrain.

11-39

Blending prairie tufts and electrostatic grass results in a realistic color and texture that you simply cannot get from ground foam alone.

bottle about 3" or 4" above the layout surface. Repeat the process until the area is covered.

One color of static grass will make your scenery look more realistic, but you can get some really neat effects by blending several colors together (**11-34**).

Silflor grass

Silflor makes numerous grass mats of various textures and colors. Although these mats may seem a little pricey, they produce stunningly realistic results, making them well worth the cost especially to highlight a special foreground scene (**11-35**).

If you measure the grass fibers on these mats with a scale rule, you'll find they're actually rather tall for all but

the wildest growth in N scale. However, the overall effect is excellent and looks great! Avoid placing figures in the taller grass, lest you never see them again!

Rather than purchase the large sheets of the material, I found I got more than what I needed from the company's small starter/sampler packs. Since Silflor is constantly introducing new products, I'd suggest carefully surveying the selection and choosing the texture, size, and color that works well for you.

No matter which you choose, the mats are applied the same way. I started by applying full-strength white glue to the areas where I wanted to have grass (**11-36**). Simply applying the grass mat to the glue won't look quite right.

Remove the mat from the package (**11-37**) and cut a small piece from the mat with scissors. With your fingers, gently pull and tease the material apart until it is very fine. I find it's easiest to actually "plant" the material in the glue with tweezers (**11-38**). When the glue dries, blend the mat into the surrounding terrain with static grass or other scenic materials, such as sifted dirt or ground foam.

Another product from Silflor, called Prairie Tufts, consist of electrostatic grass applied to a adhesive backing sheet. Peel these tufts from their backing sheet and plant them in dabs of full-strength white glue. Bunching Prairie Tufts together will duplicate the look of an overgrown pasture or meadow (**11-39**).

About the author

Marty McGuirk can trace his interest in model railroading to a Lionel train set a neighbor gave him when he was six years old. A later visit to New London, Conn., to tour U. S. Navy submarines shortly thereafter led to a cab ride on a Central Vermont locomotive, which turned into a lifelong interest in the history and operations of that line. After graduating from The Citadel, Marty spent 10 years on active duty in the U. S. Navy. While in the service, he and several friends started the Central Vermont Railway Historical Society.

Marty served as an Associate Editor at Kalmbach Publishing's *Classic Toy Trains* and *Model Railroader* magazines from 1994 to 2001 and later worked in product development for InterMountain Railway Company. He has built layouts and models in a variety of scales and gauges, including N, HO, and even Sn3. This is his third book.

Marty works as a contractor for the federal government, and he and his wife, Christine, live in the Washington, D.C., area.

Acknowledgments

I would like to thank Paul Graf at Atlas Model Railroad Co., Bill Schneider from Branchline Trains, Zana Ireland of Digitrax, Jim Elster at Scenic Express, and Kara Benson at Wm. K. Walthers for their assistance in obtaining product samples and supplies.

Bernard Kempinski gets a lot of the credit for the workable design of the Androscoggin Central layout—I came up with the basic concept, but Bernie helped flesh it out and drafted a rough operating scheme that showed the layout would be as much fun to operate as it was to build. Bernie also provided several structures, including the signature brick mill, for the layout.

I didn't want to limit the photographs of finished models and scenes to my own work, so special thanks to Bill Denton, Keith Kohlmann, Lance Mindheim, Verne Niner, and Bernie for providing some of the wonderful photographs of their own layouts and modules. I'd also like to thank Mark Thompson and Jeff Wilson at Kalmbach Books for their assistance with this project.

Finally, I thank my son Matthew for his help with everything from layout construction to computer assistance, and most of all, thanks go to Christine for all her encouragement and support, without which this book would be never have become a reality.

—*Marty McGuirk*

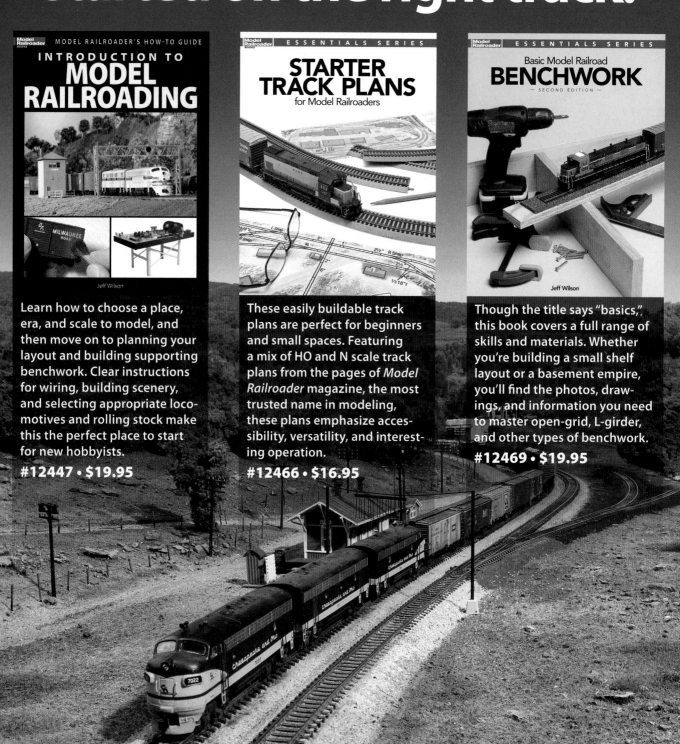

More great books to get you started on the right track!

MODEL RAILROADER'S HOW-TO GUIDE

INTRODUCTION TO MODEL RAILROADING

Jeff Wilson

Learn how to choose a place, era, and scale to model, and then move on to planning your layout and building supporting benchwork. Clear instructions for wiring, building scenery, and selecting appropriate locomotives and rolling stock make this the perfect place to start for new hobbyists.

#12447 • $19.95

ESSENTIALS SERIES

STARTER TRACK PLANS
for Model Railroaders

These easily buildable track plans are perfect for beginners and small spaces. Featuring a mix of HO and N scale track plans from the pages of *Model Railroader* magazine, the most trusted name in modeling, these plans emphasize accessibility, versatility, and interesting operation.

#12466 • $16.95

ESSENTIALS SERIES

Basic Model Railroad
BENCHWORK
— SECOND EDITION —

Jeff Wilson

Though the title says "basics," this book covers a full range of skills and materials. Whether you're building a small shelf layout or a basement empire, you'll find the photos, drawings, and information you need to master open-grid, L-girder, and other types of benchwork.

#12469 • $19.95

KB
KALMBACH BOOKS

Buy now from hobby shops! To find a store near you, visit www.HobbyRetailer.com
www.KalmbachStore.com or call 1-800-533-6644
Monday – Friday, 8:30 a.m. – 4:30 p.m. CST. Outside the United States and Canada call 262-796-8776, ext. 661.

P20007

2XMR